RAISING A BLACK SCHOLAR

A CURRICULIM

Roosevelt Mitchell III

ISBN:0990885046
ISBN-13:9780990885047

DEDICATION

This book is dedicated to our ancestors who dreamed and sacrificed for a world they knew they wouldn't benefit from by investing in their children

CONTENTS

About the Author

A Note to Parents and Teachers

General Introduction

ABOUT THE AUTHOR

Roosevelt Mitchell III is an Award Winning Educator, Author, National Speaker and Scholar. His research includes "The Hiring Practices of School Districts for African American Male Special Education Teachers." Roosevelt has written the popular children's book "Kayden is Different" to stop bullying at the elementary school level and to teach kids to accept each other's differences. He also authored "Diary of a Disability Scholar" that is used to prepare Special Education teacher candidates at the collegiate level. Roosevelt is President and Founder of the Roosevelt Mitchell III (RMIII) Foundation

A Note to Parents and Teachers

Although we list what the child should know before entering each grade level, we focus heavily on supplying the reader with free resources and links of the aspects that aren't taught in school. Most of the book is addressed and intended to be taught to African American boys and girls. However, at the beginning of each chapter we have supplied a brief introduction with advice for parents and teachers and it can certainly be applied to all children. It's our hope that the introductions and resources will be useful for parents seeking to build on the foundation of their child, and for teachers, to diversify their lesson plans to create more scholars. If you are interested in learning more about the work and ideas of Raising Black Scholars, please contact at Roosevelt Mitchell III: roosevelt@rooseveltmitchell.com

General Introduction

Raising Black Scholars Series

What is your child learning in school?

A parent recently contacted me expressing a concern about her son. She stated that he had always been an honor roll student in high school, but was struggling mightily his first year in college. How could this be? What if I told you that in some school districts your child can make the honor roll every semester and still not be prepared for college? It's true! Many parents would be surprised if they actually looked at the school district's curriculum of what their child was being taught. The vague wording used in many curricula confuses many of the teachers who are trying to teach it. Besides the deficiency in the interpretation of the curricula, legislation like "No Child Left Behind" and "Race to the Top" forces many teachers to push students through to the next grade even if they had not mastered the concepts. This results in students graduating from high school and not prepared for college or adulthood.

Why an African American curriculum is needed

American public education has been on the decline since the release of the 1983 report "A Nation at Risk." The report was issued by the National Commission on Excellence in Education that called America's educational system mediocre at best. Fast forward over thirty years later and now the United States has adopted the Common Core State Standards Initiative that states what students should know in English and Math at the end of each grade and they are able to compare progress from state to state. The Common Core doesn't fit the definition of true education either as it is filled with state testing that doesn't teach kids or inspire them to do anything but fill in bubbles. The system does nothing for African American children to raise their self-esteem, to love them, teach them self-worth, true black history to inspire them or financial literacy and entrepreneurship so they can learn how to create a job instead of how to only apply for one. An African American based curriculum provides the parent with the necessary tools to shape and mold your son or daughter into a black scholar. This curriculum bridges that gap between being just a student and becoming a black scholar. In today's society our children must be well rounded in order to compete in a global market.

Positive Self-Esteem and Self-Worth

It's impossible for black boys and girls to develop a positive sense of self when they are taught that the existence of their race began at slavery and they have historically only been butlers and the help. What's rarely mentioned is when Africans were Kings and Queens or the history of Black Wall-Street. Black history is celebrated in such a parochial lens in current curriculums and schools that black children aren't aware that black history is being made every day by black brothers and sisters all over the world. The educational system could easily empower our babies by teaching more positive black imagery instead of consistently reminding them that blacks were second class citizens. This curriculum has African American historical figures and links at each grade level that seeks to empower black boys and girls. It begins teaching pre-kindergartens about when black people were Kings and Queens in Africa and ends with teaching high school seniors about current people of color all over the world that are achieving amazing things. This strategy seduces black boys and girls into a level of excellence so they will no longer accept mediocrity.

Mental Health

A study published in the JAMA Pediatrics recently found that the suicide rate among black boys has doubled since 1993. The suicide rate among white children during the same period has declined. The study tracked the suicide rate of children aged 5 to 11 from 1993 to 2012. During the period studied, the suicide rate among black boys rose from 1.78 to 3.47 per million, while suicides among white boys dropped from 1.96 to 1.31 per million. Black parents have to be more hands on more than ever in help shaping their child's self-esteem and self-worth. The confidence and self-worth must be instilled at home because the school system is not going to do it. Nationally less than fifteen percent of teachers are black and most of them are woman. Only two percent of teachers nationwide are black men. What effect does that have on black kids? Department of Education reported in 2012 the impact of school discipline policies effect black students three and a half times more that White students, as they are more likely to be suspended or expelled than their white peers. How can a child have positive self-esteem in a place that they are misunderstood and viewed as a problem? In this curriculum we provide links and resources to help strengthen our black boys and girls mental health and combat the psychological preparation of the school to prison pipeline.

Financial Literacy and Entrepreneurship

There are more black millionaires and billionaires in the black community than ever before. As this is reality we are also experiencing a large and increasing gap between the rich and the rest of us. As society loves to celebrate the net worth of the first black female billionaire, Oprah Winfrey, ironically the current median wealth of single black women in the prime of their working years (ages 36 to 49) is a measly five dollars. While white women of the same age group current median wealth is about $42,600. With those statistics no one can argue the point that while only a few blacks are doing great, the masses are struggling mightily. How can the black community reverse these horrible statistics? Educating our children on financial literacy and teaching them how to create a job instead of begging for one, that's how! Andrew Young stated "Martin Luther King Jr. and I integrated the lunch counter, but we never integrated the dollar. And to live in a system of free enterprise, and yet not to understand the rules of free enterprise, that's the definition of slavery." With this curriculum we are picking up the baton where Andrew Young and Dr. King passed it on. In this Raising Black Scholar curriculum we are creating scholars who are going to improve our communities, create businesses, create economic empowerment and build wealth.

PRE- K Curriculum

Introduction

According to the Center for Public Education a large and growing body of research shows that investing in high-quality pre-kindergarten education yields benefits for children, schools, and communities. Evidence also indicates that children who engage in high quality pre-k curriculums enter school ahead of their peers who did not. So this stage is highly important as the foundation is laid to which the rest of the child's learning experience will be built upon. At this age pediatricians and psychologists encourage parents to teach their children the correct words for their genitalia and when to tell them when these places has been touched in order to prevent sexual crimes. Most sexual crimes are committed on children by people they know and family members so teaching bodily autonomy is important at this stage.

Before entering Kindergarten the student should be able to:

1) Be able to state first and last name when asked.
2) Be able to write first name with first letter upper case and remaining letters lower case.
3) Use appropriate three-finger grasp when using writing instruments (pencils, crayons and scissors)
4) Count to at least ten and tell what number comes before or after a given number to 10.
5) Know all the letters in their first name.
6) Identify basic geometric shapes (triangle, circle, square, rectangle, oval, star, rhombus (diamond) and heart)

7) Know basic colors (red, blue, green, yellow, orange, purple, black, white, brown, pink)

8) Identify numerals 1-10 in random order.

9) Make most letter/sound matches.

10) Identify most upper and lower case letters.

11) Use finger to accurately touch count items to ten.

12) Knows concepts of print (front and back of book, which page comes first, track words left to right).

13) Be able to rhyme words.

14) Retells simple stories in sequence.

15) When given a word ("man") and a new beginning sound (/f/), creates the familiar word ("fan")

16) Recognize Preschool Dolch Wordlist- (50-75% of all words used in school books, library books, newspapers, and magazines are in the Dolch Basic Sight Vocabulary of 220 words (preschool thru Grade 3).

Set 1	Set II	SET III
a	away	find
can	Little	funny
here	my	help
is	run	jump
said	we	one
and	come	two
for	look	three
I	not	blue
it	see	read
the	where	yellow
big	down	
go	make	
in	play	
me	up	
To	You	

Resources (Worksheets and Printable)

1) http://www.education.com/worksheets/preschool/
2) www.tlsbooks.com/preschoolnumberandpremathworksheets.htm
3) www.kidzone.ws
4) http://www.sheppardsoftware.com/preschool/preschool.htm
5) http://www.internet4classrooms.com/early_childhood/alphabet_pre-k.htm

Speech and Language IPAD Apps

- ✓ Artic Pix
- ✓ Kaufman Cards
- ✓ Speech Tutor
- ✓ Talking Tom
- ✓ WH Questions
- ✓ Conversation Builder

Math IPAD Apps

- ✓ Splash Math
- ✓ Counting and Addition! Math and Numbers educational games by i Learn With
- ✓ Math is fun: Age 4-5

Cause & Effect IPAD Apps

- ✓ Firework
- ✓ I Hear Ewe
- ✓ Alexicom AAC

African American Historical Figures

1. **PIANKHY: Conqueror of Egypt**

   http://www.ijebu.org/conquerors/piankhy/

2. **ANTAR: Afro-Arabian Poet-Story Teller**

   http://margariaziza.com/2007/12/24/the-black-knight-antar-and-the-arab-epic/

3. **SONNI ALI: Founder of Songhay**

   http://www.britannica.com/EBchecked/topic/554537/Sonni-Ali

4. **ASKIA The Great: Builder of Songhay**

   http://www.blackpast.org/gah/toure-muhammad-c-1442-1538

5. **ABRAM HANNIBAL: Solider, Commander in Russia**

   http://www.aaregistry.org/historic_events/view/slave-general-abram-hannibal

6. **Chaka: 18th Century Zulu King and Warrior**

   http://en.wikipedia.org/wiki/Zulu_Kingdom

7. **Gustavus Vassa: Seafarer, Colonizer**

   http://www.brycchancarey.com/equiano/

8. **Joseph Cinque: African Prince and Revolutionist**

   http://spartacus-educational.com/Scinque.htm

9. **Menelik II: Founder of Modern Ethiopia**

   http://en.wikipedia.org/wiki/Menelik_II

African American Preschool Books

1) Shoebox Sam By: Mary Brigid Barrett

2) Let it Shine: Three Favorite Spirituals by: Ashley Bryan

3) Flower Garden by: Eve Bunting

4) Kente Colors by: Debbi Chocolate

5) Full, Full, Full of Love by: Trish Cooke

6) My Family Plays Music by: Judy Cox

7) The Neighborhood Mother Goose by: Nina Crews

8) Rap A Tap Tap by: Leo Dillon

9) This Jazz Man by: Karen Ehrhardt

10) Hot Day on Abbott Avenue by: Karen English

11) Summer Jackson: Grown Up by: Teresa E Harris

12) Black All Around! by: Patricia Hubbell

13) My People by Langston Hughes

14) Lily Brown's Paintings by: Angela Johnson

15) Keisha Ann Can! By: Daniel Kirk

16) This Little Light of Mine by: Earl B Lewis

17) Lola Loves Stories by: Anna McQuinn

18) He's Got the Whole World in His Hands by: Kadir Nelson

19) All Aboard! By: Mary Lyn Ray

20) Back of the Bus by: Aaron Reynolds

21) My Nana and Me by: Irene Smalls

22) The Hat that Wore Clara B. by: Melanie Turner-Denstaedt

23) Pecan Pie Baby by: Jacqueline Woodson

24) Lucky Beans by: Becky Birtha

25) Kayden is Different by: Roosevelt Mitchell III, M.Ed.

Sample Lesson Plan

The lesson plan below is just a sample because all kids learn at different speeds and as the parent; YOU determine when your child has mastered the concept and when it's time to introduce the next concept. Here are a few tips:

Keys to learning

- ➢ Read to child EVERDAY
- ➢ Introduce new skill and provide lots of practice
- ➢ Reinforcement of Concept (Continue to build on concepts)
- ➢ Repetition (practice, practice, practice)
- ➢ Keep child engaged (manipulatives and games)

Activity	Monday	Tuesday	Wednesday	Thursday	Friday
Representational (Literacy)	Read book to child	Read book to child	Read book to child	Read book to child	Read book to child
Cognitive (Math)	Introduce the number "ONE"	***Practice Concept** -Use manipulative (blocks, toys)	***Practice Concept** Integrate technology (Use IPAD game)	***Practice Concept** -Use manipulative (food, shoes)	***Practice Concept** Integrate technology (Use IPAD game)
Social Emotional (social studies/science)	-Introduce the letter "A" and "a"	***Practice Concept** -writing worksheet of letter "A" and "a" (Print a worksheet from one of websites)	***Practice Concept** Integrate technology (Use IPAD game)	***Practice Concept** -writing worksheet of letter "A" and "a" (Print a worksheet from one of websites)	***Practice Concept** Integrate technology (Use IPAD game)
Physical Development	Introduce how to correctly hold a pencil and crayon	***Practice Concept** -trace the number "1"	***Practice Concept** Integrate technology (Use IPAD game)	***Practice Concept** -trace the number "1"	***Practice Concept** Integrate technology (Use IPAD game)

NOTES

....

....

....

....

....

....

....

....

....

....

....

....

....

....

....

....

NOTES

NOTES

Kindergarten Curriculum

Introduction

In kindergarten children should grow socially and emotionally but most importantly their self-confidence should be established. When a child's self-confidence is raised it increases their self-esteem which in turn improves the child's mental health. Self-awareness teaches kids how they see themselves and understand how others view them. All of these things are important for black boys and girls as the enter spaces in society where institutional racism still exist. A study done by Stanford University has unveiled some disturbing facts: a Black student is likely to be punished more harshly than a White student. The discipline gap within schools consequently makes a lot of black boys and girls have low self-esteem and low self-confidence.

This results in kids becoming less effective learners and hinders social and skill development. We have included links in this chapter that helps build your child's self-esteem and self-awareness.

Before entering the 1st grade the student should be able to:

1) Know all the letters of the alphabet
2) How to connect sounds with letters
3) Recognize sight words (such as I, a, me, are, see, like, and, etc.)
4) Read 25 books for pleasure and gather information
5) Understand how words work by following along while he or she listens to simple books
6) Follow simple directions
7) Write independently

8) Tell stories or ideas to an adult

9) Print numbers, letters of the alphabet and a few simple words.

10) Write numbers from 0 to 21 in order

11) Count aloud to 100, backwards from 10, and by 10's to 100

12) Build addition and subtraction families to 5 (for example, 2+3=5, 1+4=5, 5-3=2, etc.)

13) Recognize the names of squares, rectangles, circles and triangles

14) Measure objects using non-standard units (for example, the table is four teddy bears high)

15) Use the terms "longer," "shorter," "equal," "more" and "less."

16) Recognize and name pennies, nickels, dimes, quarters, and their values.

17) Recognize simples patterns (such as a/b/a/c or red/yellow/red/blue)

18) Read and interpret graphs

19) Recognize Kindergarten Dolch Wordlist- (50-75% of all words used in school books, library books, newspapers, and magazines are in the Dolch Basic Sight Vocabulary of 220 words (preschool thru Grade 3).

Set 1	Set 2	Set 3	Set 4
All	Am	Are	At
Ate	Be	Black	Brown
But	Came	Did	Do
Eat	Four	Get	Good
Have	He	Into	Like
Must	New	No	Now
On	Our	Out	Please
Pretty	Ran	Ride	Saw
Say	She	So	Soon
That	There	They	This
Too	Under	Want	Was
Well	Went	What	White
Who	Will	With	Yes

Self- Esteem

1) **Developing Your Child's Self-esteem**

   http://kidshealth.org/parent/emotions/feelings/self_esteem.html

2) **Helping Your Child Develop A Healthy Sense of Self Esteem**

   https://www.healthychildren.org/English/ages-stages/gradeschool/Pages/Helping-Your-Child-Develop-A-Healthy-Sense-of-Self-Esteem.aspx

3) **10 Ways to Build Self-Esteem in Black Girls**

   http://babyandblog.com/2014/03/10-ways-to-build-self-esteem-in-black-girls/

4) **Building self-esteem: children 1-8 years**

   http://raisingchildren.net.au/articles/self-esteem_different_ages.html

5) **Ten ways to build your child's self-esteem**

   http://www.babycenter.com/0_ten-ways-to-build-your-childs-self-esteem_65569.bc

Resources (Worksheets and Printable)

1) http://www.education.com/worksheets/kindergarten/

2) http://www.tlsbooks.com/kindergartenworksheets.htm

3) www.kidzone.ws

4) http://www.sheppardsoftware.com

5) http://www.internet4classrooms.com/kindergarten_links.htm

Speech and Language IPAD Apps

✓ Artic Pix
✓ Kaufman Cards
✓ Speech Tutor
✓ Talking Tom
✓ WH Questions
✓ Conversation Builder

Math Apps

- ✓ Splash Math
- ✓ Counting and Addition! Math and Numbers educational games by i Learn With
- ✓ Math is fun: Age 4-5

Cause & Effect Apps

- ✓ Firework
- ✓ I Hear Ewe
- ✓ Alexicom AAC

African American Historical Figures

1. **Hank Aaron**

   http://www.biography.com/people/hank-aaron-9173497

2. **Kareem Abdul-Jabbar**

   http://www.biography.com/people/kareem-abdul-jabbar-9174053

3. **Muhammed Ali**

   http://www.biography.com/people/muhammad-ali-9181165

4. **Charles Barkley**

   http://www.biography.com/people/charles-barkley-9542575

5. **Wilt Chamberlain**

   http://www.biography.com/people/wilt-chamberlain-9243766

6. **Reggie Jackson**

   http://www.biography.com/people/reggie-jackson-9351402

7. **Michael Jordan**

   http://www.biography.com/people/michael-jordan-9358066

8. **Jackie Joyner- Kersee**

   http://www.biography.com/people/jackie-joyner-kersee-9358710

9. **Sugar Ray Leonard**

   http://www.biography.com/people/sugar-ray-leonard-9379459

10. **Joe Louis**

    http://www.biography.com/people/joe-louis-9386989

11. **Jesse Owens**

   http://www.biography.com/people/jesse-owens-9431142

12. **Maya Angelou**

   http://www.biography.com/people/maya-angelou-9185388

13. **Ralph Ellison**

   http://www.biography.com/people/ralph-ellison-9286702

14. **Alex Haley**

   http://www.biography.com/people/alex-haley-39420

15. **Lorraine Hansberry**

   http://www.biography.com/people/lorraine-hansberry-9327823

16. **Langston Hughes**

   http://www.biography.com/people/langston-hughes-9346313

17. **Zora Neale Hurston**

   http://www.biography.com/people/zora-neale-hurston-9347659

18. **Walter Mosley**

   http://www.biography.com/people/walter-mosley-38445

19. **Richard Wright**

   http://www.biography.com/people/richard-wright-9537751

20. **Ella Baker**

   http://www.biography.com/people/ella-baker-9195848

21. **Stokely Carmichael**

   http://www.biography.com/people/stokely-carmichael-9238629

22. **W.E.B. DuBois**

   http://www.biography.com/people/web-du-bois-9279924

23. **Medgar Evers**

   http://www.biography.com/people/medgar-evers-9542324

24. **Marcus Garvey**

   http://www.biography.com/people/marcus-garvey-9307319

25. **Martin Luther King Jr.**

   http://www.biography.com/people/martin-luther-king-jr-9365086

African American Kindergarten Books

1. Cornrows by Camille Yarbrough
2. Wild, Wild Hair (level 3) (Hello Reader) by Nikki Grimes
3. I Love My Hair! by Natasha Tarpley
4. Nappy Hair (Dragonfly Books) by Joe Cepeda
5. Happy to Be Nappy (Jump at the Sun) by Bell Hooks
6. Shades of Black: A Celebration of Our Children by Sandra L. Pinkney
7. Bintou's Braids by Sylviane A. Diouf
8. Bigmama's by Donald Crews
9. Kids Talk Hair: An Instruction Book for Grown-Ups & Kids by Pamela Ferrell
10. My Aunt Came Back (Harper Growing Tree) by Pat Cummings
11. The Day I Was Rich (Little Bill) by Bill Cosby
12. Grandpa, Is Everything Black Bad? by Sandy Lynne Holman
13. The Gifts of Kwanzaa by Synthia Saint James
14. My Hair Is Beautiful: Because Its Mine (Black Butterfly Board Books) by Paula Dejoie
15. Something Beautiful by Sharon Dennis Wyeth
16. Come On, Rain! by Karen Hesse
17. Colors Come from God . . . Just Like Me! by Carolyn A. Forché
18. Pretty Brown Face by Andrea Davis Pinkney
19. Bright Eyes, Brown Skin (A Feeling Good Book) (A Feeling Good Book) by Cheryl Willis Hudson
20. Good Morning, Baby (What a Baby) by Cheryl Willis Hudson

Lesson Plan

The lesson plan below is just a sample because all kids learn at different speeds and as the parent; YOU determine when your child has mastered the concept and when it's time to introduce the next concept. Here are a few tips:

KEYS TO LEARNING

- ➢ Read to child EVERDAY
- ➢ Introduce new skill and provide lots of practice
- ➢ Reinforcement of Concept (Continue to add new concepts and continue to use the old one)
- ➢ Repetition (practice, practice, practice)
- ➢ Keep child engaged (use mixture of manipulative and games)

Sample Lesson Plan

Activity	Monday	Tuesday	Wednesday	Thursday	Friday
Representational (Literacy)	Read book to child	Read book to child	Read book to child	Read book to child	Read book to child
Cognitive (Math)	Introduce Concept	***Practice Concept** -Use manipulative (blocks, toys)	***Practice Concept** Integrate technology (Use IPAD game)	***Practice Concept** -Use manipulative (food, shoes)	***Practice Concept** Integrate technology (Use IPAD game)
Social Emotional (social studies/science)	Introduce Concept	***Practice Concept**	***Practice Concept** Integrate technology (Use IPAD game)	***Practice Concept**	***Practice Concept** Integrate technology (Use IPAD game)
Physical Development	Introduce Concept	***Practice Concept**	***Practice Concept** Integrate technology (Use IPAD game)	***Practice Concept**	***Practice Concept** Integrate technology (Use IPAD game)

NOTES

....

....

....

....

....

....

NOTES

_____

_____

_____

_____

_____

_____

_____

_____

NOTES

1st Grade Curriculum

Introduction

According to the research in an article published on the Harvard Graduate School of Education website, academic success can be determined starting in first grade. First grade is also the stage that kids should be able to communicate verbally their feelings and needs in a decent manner. Being integrated in a large school for the first time they must be able to apply coping skills in this new environment. Therefore first grade is a litmus test and measuring tool that parents can use to gauge what needs to be continued or discontinued. This is a critical time that parents take the time out and review all of the things that your child should be able to do up to this point. What typically happens in the school setting is that students are pushed to the next grade without mastering the grade level objectives and it's almost impossible for them to catch up. In the earlier lessons we presented IPAD or smart phone apps that the child could use to introduce him or her to technology. Now it is time to introduce your child to the internet and search engines. Show them how to navigate the internet and let them spend free time on it daily exploring and getting used to it. Our kids are competing in a global economy and our children must be fluent in technology in order to compete at a high level. This chapter includes links for mentoring organizations, coping strategies for kids and links for building self-esteem and self-worth.

KEY POINTS

- Make child read EVERDAY

- Coping Strategies

- Introduce to Internet and Search Engines

- Continue Sex Education

- Build Self-esteem and Self-worth

- Financial Literacy

Before entering the 2nd grade the student should be able to:

1) Work independently at desk

2) Listen to longer sets of directions

3) Read directions off the board, although some children may still have difficulty with this

4) Complete homework and bring it back the next day

5) Sit in a chair for a longer period of time

6) Be able to see things from another person's point of view so you can reason with your child and teach her empathy

7) Relate to and repeat experiences in greater detail and in a logical way after listening

8) Problem-solve disagreements

9) Crave affection from parents and teachers

10) Have some minor difficulties with friendships and working out problems with peers

11) Distinguish left from right

12) Be able to plan ahead

13) Write and spell untaught words phonetically

14) Read and write high-frequency words such as *where* and *every*

15) Write complete sentences with correct capitalization and punctuation

16) Understand and use correctly conjunctions and prepositions, such as *but* and *beyond*

17) Read aloud first-grade books with accuracy and understanding

18) Tell time to the hour and half-hour using analog and digital clocks

19) Quickly answer addition problems with sums up to 20

20) Quickly answer subtraction problems with numbers 0 to 20

21) Complete two-digit addition and subtraction problems without regrouping

22) Recognize 1ˢᵗ grade Dolch Wordlist- (50-75% of all words used in school books, library books, newspapers, and magazines are in the Dolch Basic Sight Vocabulary of 220 words (preschool thru Grade 3).

after	again	an
any	as	ask
by	could	every
fly	from	give
giving	had	has

her	him	his
how	may	of
once	open	over
some	stop	take
them	then	walk

just	know	let
live	old	put
round	thank	think
were	when	
five	5	

Resources (Worksheets and Printable)

1) http://www.education.com
2) http://www.tlsbooks.com
3) www.kidzone.ws
4) http://www.sheppardsoftware.com
5) http://www.internet4classrooms.com

Speech and Language Apps

✓ Artic Pix
✓ Kaufman Cards
✓ Speech Tutor
✓ Talking Tom
✓ WH Questions
✓ Conversation Builder

Math Apps

✓ Counting Money
✓ Counting Bills & Coins
✓ Splash Math
✓ Math Express
✓ Counting and Addition! Math and Numbers educational games by i Learn With

Personal Finance

1. **Barter vs Money**

   http://www.takechargeamerica.org/wp-content/themes/tca/pdfs/teaching-resources/grade-one-barter-vs-money.pdf

2. **Wants and Needs**

   http://www.takechargeamerica.org/wp-content/themes/tca/pdfs/teaching-resources/grade-one-wants-and-needs.pdf

3. **Saving Money**

   http://www.takechargeamerica.org/wp-content/themes/tca/pdfs/teaching-resources/grade-one-saving-money.pdf

4. **Price**

   http://www.takechargeamerica.org/wp-content/themes/tca/pdfs/teaching-resources/grade-one-price.pdf

5. **Jobs**

   http://www.takechargeamerica.org/wp-content/themes/tca/pdfs/teaching-resources/grade-one-jobs.pdf

6. **It's on Sale**

   http://www.takechargeamerica.org/wp-content/themes/tca/pdfs/teaching-resources/grade-one-its-on-sale.pdf

7. **How Much How Many**

   http://www.takechargeamerica.org/wp-content/themes/tca/pdfs/teaching-resources/grade-one-how-much-how-many.pdf

8. **Savings Accounts and Interest**

   http://www.takechargeamerica.org/wp-content/themes/tca/pdfs/teaching-resources/grade-one-savings-accounts-and-interest.pdf

9. **Shopping**

   http://www.takechargeamerica.org/wp-content/themes/tca/pdfs/teaching-resources/grade-one-shopping.pdf

Sex Education Discussion Topics

1) Where babies come from

2) Body parts/functions

3) Male/female differences, roles, and expectations

4) Sexual language

Building Self-esteem and Self-worth

1. **How to Build Self-Worth**

   http://www.wikihow.com/Build-Self-Worth

2. **Building Self-esteem in your kids**

   http://www.focusonthefamily.com/parenting/effective-biblical-discipline/why-kids-misbehave/building-selfesteem-in-your-kids

3. **Positive Parenting Tips Building Your Child's Self-Esteem**

   http://islamic-world.net/parenting/parenting_page/positive_parenting_tips4.htm

4. **Building Self-Esteem Activities**

   http://kidshealth.org/classroom/prekto2/personal/growing/self_esteem.pdf

5. **Self-esteem: How to Help Children & Teens Develop a Positive Self-image**

   http://childdevelopmentinfo.com/child-psychology/self-esteem/

Coping Skills

1. **Teaching Coping Skills**

   http://www.pbisworld.com/tier-1/teach-coping-skills/

2. **Coping Skills for Managing Emotions**

   https://www.kidsmatter.edu.au/families/about-emotions/childrens-emotions/coping-skills-managing-emotions

3. **Coping Skills Activities**

   https://www.pinterest.com/explore/coping-skills-activities/

African American Historical Figures

1. **Estavanico: Arizona's African Discoverer**

   http://originalpeople.org/estevanico-african-born-man-who-explored-mexico-and-arizona-in-the-early-1500s/

2. **L'Ouverture, Dessalines, Christophe: Hatiti: Three Who Made Revolution**

   http://www.blackpast.org/gah/loverture-toussaint-1742-1803

3. **Crispus Attucks: First to Die for Independence-**

   http://www.crispusattucksmuseum.org/crispus-attucks/

4. **Peter Salem: Black Hero of Bunker Hill**

   http://www.celebrateboston.com/biography/peter-salem.htm

5. **Oliver Cromwell: With Washington at Delaware**

   http://encyclopedia.jrank.org/articles/pages/4183/Cromwell-Oliver-1752-1853.html

6. **Benjamin Banneker: Mathematical Wizard and Inventor**

   http://www.bnl.gov/bera/activities/globe/banneker.htm

7. **Jean Baptiste Pointe De Sable: Chicago's First Settler**

   http://www.pbs.org/wgbh/amex/chicago/peopleevents/p_dusable.html

8. **Prince Hall: Fraternal Leader**

   http://en.wikipedia.org/wiki/Prince_Hall

9. **Paul Cuffe: Early Businessman and Colonizer**

   http://www.blackpast.org/aah/cuffe-paul-sr-1759-1817

10. **James Forten: Forgotten Abolitionist**

    http://www.biography.com/people/james-forten-9299324

11. **Denmark Vesey: Anti-Slavery Insurrectionist**

    http://www.britannica.com/EBchecked/topic/626831/Denmark-Vesey

12. **David Walker: Appeal to the Slaves**

    http://docsouth.unc.edu/nc/walker/bio.html

13. **Nat Turner: Anti-Slavery Revolutionist**

    http://www.biography.com/people/nat-turner-9512211

14. **William Still: Underground Railroad Leader**

    http://stillfamily.library.temple.edu/historical-perspective/william-still-significance

15. **Harriet Tubman: Black Moses of Her Race**

    http://www.harriettubman.com/callhermoses.html

16. **Sojourner Truth: A Pilgrim of Freedom**

    http://biography.yourdictionary.com/sojourner-truth

17. Frederick A. Douglass: Golden Trombone of Abolition

http://www.biography.com/people/frederick-douglass-9278324

18. James P. Beckwourth: Western Frontiersman

http://americacomesalive.com/2013/02/10/james-pierson-beckwourth-1798-1866-explorer-and-frontiersman/#.VWpZ9s9Viko

19. Alexander Crummell: Writer, Advocate of Equality, Minister

http://www.biography.com/people/alexander-crummell-37889

20. Robert Smalls: Navigator, Slave-Hero, Congressman

http://www.aaregistry.org/historic_events/view/naval-hero-and-politician-robert-smalls

21. Hiriam Revels: U.S, Senator from Mississippi

http://www.biography.com/people/hiram-r-revels-9456129

22. Blanche K Bruce: Senator from Mississippi

http://www.biography.com/people/blanche-k-bruce-37324

23. Robert B. Elliott: U.S. Congressman from South Carolina

http://bioguide.congress.gov/scripts/biodisplay.pl?index=E000128

24. Richard H. Cain: U.S. Congressman from South Carolina

http://bioguide.congress.gov/scripts/biodisplay.pl?index=c000022

25. John R. Lynch: U.S. Congressman from Mississippi

http://www.biography.com/people/john-r-lynch-37635#synopsis

African American 1st Grade Books

1. Good Night, Baby (revised) (What a Baby) by Cheryl Willis Hudson

2. The Snowy Day by Ezra Jack Keats

3. Cheetah Girls, The: It's Raining Benjamins - Book #6 by Deborah Gregory

4. Cassie's Colorful Day: A Tar Beach Board Book (Tar Beach Board Books) by Faith Ringgold

5. The Princess Who Lost Her Hair: An Akamba Legend (Legends of the World) by Tololwa M. Mollel

6. The Other Side *by* Jacqueline Woodson

7. Minty: A Story of Young Harriet Tubman *by* Alan Schroeder

8. Martin's Big Words: The Life of Dr. Martin Luther King Jr. *by* Doreen Rappaport

9. Henry's Freedom Box: A True Story from the Underground Railroad *by* Ellen Levine

10. Harlem *by* Walter Dean Myers

11. Follow the Drinking Gourd: A Story of the Underground Railroad *by* Jeanette Winter

12. Escape North!: The Story of Harriet Tubman Series: Step into Reading — 3 *by* Monica Kulling

13. Dinner at Aunt Connie's House *by* Faith Ringgold

14. Dad, Jackie, and Me *by* Myron Uhlberg

15. Addy Learns a Lesson: A School Story Series: American Girl *by* Connie Rose Porter

16. Yesterday I Had the Blues by Jeron Ashford Frame

17. Aunt Flossie's Hats and Crab Cakes Later by Elizabeth Fitzgerald Howard

18. Goin' Someplace Special by Patricia McKissak

19. Fishing Day by Andrea Davis Pinkney

NOTES

....

....

....

....

....

....

NOTES

_____

_____

_____

_____

_____

_____

_____

_____

2nd Grade Curriculum

Introduction

In second grade students began to write and read on a deeper level. They began reading longer and more complicated books and complete creative writing assignments. This stage is important that children's creative thinking and writing skills are honed through lots of practice based around their interest. It's a good idea for kid's to begin keeping a daily journal and to read simple poems and literature to spark their creativity. Continue to build your child's self-confidence and self-esteem. This is a key stage in the financial literacy development because before entering third grade they should understand concepts such as: buying, comparison shopping, keeping track of money, counting change and changing coins, managing money, market prices, savings and budget. Giving your child a fake checkbook to fill out is a great way to familiarize them with keeping track of money. This chapter includes links for coping strategies for kids and links for building self-esteem and self-worth. Lesson plans, free apps and links for buying, comparison shopping, keeping track of money, counting change and changing coins, managing money, market prices, savings and budget.

KEYS POINTS

- Make child read EVERDAY
- Start a Journal
- Coping Strategies
- Spend more time on the Internet
- Continue Sex Education

- Build Self-confidence
- Personal Finance

Before entering the 3rd grade the student should be able to:

5) Begin to reason and concentrate

6) Improve the ability to process information

7) Improve focus on a specific task

8) Work cooperatively with a partner or small group

9) Understand the difference between right and wrong

10) Make connections between concepts so child will be better able to compare and contrast ideas

11) Expand their vocabulary

12) Correctly use irregular verbs

13) Read fluently with expression

14) Ask and answer who, what, where, when, why, and how questions about a piece of reading

15) Revise and edit a piece of writing

16) Use an apostrophe to form contractions and frequently occurring possessives

17) Recognize most irregularly spelled words such as because and upon

18) Begin to use a dictionary

19) Do mental math for single-digit addition and subtraction problems

20) Add single- and multi-digit numbers with regrouping

21) Demonstrate an understanding of place value

22) Tell time to the nearest five minutes, using AM and PM

23) Know the basic concept of multiplication (for example, 2 x 3 is two rows of three and 600 is six 100s)

24) Recognize 2nd grade Dolch Wordlist- (50-75% of all words used in school books, library books, newspapers, and magazines are in the Dolch Basic Sight Vocabulary of 220 words (preschool thru Grade 3).

always	around	because
been	before	best
both	buy	call
cold	does	don't
fast	first	found

gave	goes	its
made	many	off
or	pull	read
sing	sit	sleep
tell	upon	write

right	their	these
those	us	use
very	wash	which
why	wish	work
would	your	green

right	their	these
those	us	use
very	wash	which
why	wish	work
would	your	green

Links for Educational Material

1) http://www.education.com

2) http://www.tlsbooks.com

3) www.kidzone.ws

4) http://www.sheppardsoftware.com

5) http://www.internet4classrooms.com

6) http://www.education.com/activity/second-grade/writing/

7) https://www.pinterest.com/abbiebart3/second-grade-writing-ideas/

8) http://www.writingprompts.net/2nd-grade/

Money Apps for Kids

- P2KMoney
- Kids Money
- Save! The Game
- Planet Orange
- Savings Quest
- Rich Kid Smart Kid
- H.I.P. Pocket Change
- PBS Kids Mad Money Game

Speech and Language Apps

- ✓ Artic Pix
- ✓ Kaufman Cards
- ✓ Speech Tutor
- ✓ Talking Tom

- ✓ WH Questions
- ✓ Conversation Builder

Math Apps

- ✓ Counting Money
- ✓ Counting Bills & Coins
- ✓ Splash Math
- ✓ Math Express
- ✓ Counting and Addition! Math and Numbers educational games by i Learn With

Sex Education Discussion Topics

- Correct body part names for the male and female anatomy
- Understand that all living things reproduce
- All people have the right not to be touched
- Identify different kinds of family structures
- Explain why bullying and teasing is wrong

Building Self-esteem and Self-worth

1. **How to Build Self-Worth**

   http://www.wikihow.com/Build-Self-Worth

2. **Building Self-esteem in your kids**

   http://www.focusonthefamily.com/parenting/effective-biblical-discipline/why-kids-misbehave/building-selfesteem-in-your-kids

3. **Positive Parenting Tips Building Your Child's Self-Esteem**

   http://islamic-world.net/parenting/parenting_page/positive_parenting_tips4.htm

4. **Building Self-Esteem Activities**

   http://kidshealth.org/classroom/prekto2/personal/growing/self_esteem.pdf

5. **Self-esteem: How to Help Children & Teens Develop a Positive Self-image**

   http://childdevelopmentinfo.com/child-psychology/self-esteem/

Coping Skills

1. **Teaching Coping Skills**

   http://www.pbisworld.com/tier-1/teach-coping-skills/

2. Coping Skills for Managing Emotions

> https://www.kidsmatter.edu.au/families/about-emotions/childrens-emotions/coping-skills-managing-emotions

3. Coping Skills Activities

> https://www.pinterest.com/explore/coping-skills-activities/

African American Historical Figures

1. Jefferson Long: U.S. Congressman from Georgia-

   http://www.georgiaencyclopedia.org/articles/history-archaeology/jefferson-franklin-long-1836-1901

2. John Mercer Langston: U.S. Congressman From Virginia

   http://www.biography.com/people/john-mercer-langston-9373265

3. James T. Rapier: Congressman from Alabama

   http://www.biography.com/people/james-t-rapier-40910

4. Ebenezer D. Bassett: First Negro Diplomat

   http://diplomacy.state.gov/discoverdiplomacy/explorer/peoplehistorical/169797.htm

5. Henry Highland Garnett: Abolitionist, Minister to Liberia

   http://www.biography.com/people/henry-highland-garnet-39704

6. John B. Russwurm: First Editor-Publisher

   http://en.wikipedia.org/wiki/John_Brown_Russwurm

7. John H. Smythe: U.S. Minister to Liberia

   http://www.blackpast.org/1895-john-h-smyth-african-africa-and-african-america

8. James Monroe Trotter: Recorder of Deeds

   http://slavery.monticello.org/getting-word/people/james-monroe-trotter

9. Jonathan J. Wright: South Carolina Jurist

   http://www.blackpast.org/aah/wright-jonathan-j-1840-1885

10. George W. Williams: Solider, Diplomat, Historian

    http://www.ohiohistorycentral.org/w/George_W._Williams

11. Pinckney Benton Stewart Pinchback: Lt. Governor of Louisiana

    http://www.biography.com/people/pinckney-pinchback-9440897

12. **Elijah McCoy: "The Real McCoy"**

    http://www.enchantedlearning.com/inventors/page/m/mccoy.shtml

13. **Norbert Rillieux: Slave, Scientist**

    https://webfiles.uci.edu/mcbrown/display/rillieux.html

14. **Jan Ernst Matzeliger: Inventor and Businessman**

    http://www.biography.com/people/jan-matzeliger-21317107#synopsis

15. **Granville T. Woods: Prolific Inventor**

    http://www.usasciencefestival.org/schoolprograms/2014-role-models-in-science-engineering/448-granville-t.html

16. **Garrett A. Morgan: Inventor for Safety**

    http://www.biography.com/people/garrett-morgan-9414691

17. **Martin R. Delany: Ethnologist**

    http://www.blackpast.org/aah/delany-major-martin-robison-1812-1885

18. **Matthew A. Henson: Polar Explorer**

    http://www.biography.com/people/matthew-henson-9335648

19. **George Washington Carver: Savior of Southern Agriculture**

    https://www.cpp.edu/~nova/scientists/articles/carver.html

20. **Daniel Hale Williams: First Successful Heart Surgeon**

    http://www.biography.com/people/daniel-hale-williams-9532269

21. **Ernest E. Just: Biologist**

    http://www.biography.com/people/ernest-everett-just-9359195

22. **Ulysses Grant Dailey: Surgeon**

    http://en.wikipedia.org/wiki/Ulysses_Grant_Dailey

23. **Charles Drew: Pioneer in Blood Plasma Research**

    http://www.biography.com/people/charles-drew-9279094

24. **Percy Julian: Chemist**

    http://www.biography.com/people/percy-julian-9359018

25. **Theodore K. Lawless**

    http://www.blackhistoryheroes.com/2010/02/dr-theodore-kenneth-lawless.html

African American 2nd Grade Books

1. **The Bat Boy and His Violin** by Curtis Gavin

2. **Catching the Moon: The Story of a Young Girl's Baseball Dream** by Crystal Hubbard

3. **Wind Flyers** by Angela Johnson

4. **A Pride of African Tales** by Donna L. Washington

5. **Dear Mr. Rosenwald** by Carole Boston Weatherford

6. **Jabberwocky** by Lewis Carroll

7. **Precious and the Boo Hag** by Patricia C. McKissack, Onawumi Jean Moss

8. **Henry's Freedom Box** by Ellen Levine

9. **The Escape of Oney Judge: Martha Washington's Slave Finds Freedom** by Emily Arnold McCully

10. **Nothing But Trouble: The Story of Althea Gibson** by Sue Stauffacher

11. **Crossing Bok Chitto: A Choctaw Tale of Friendship and Freedom** by Tim Tingle

12. **Freedom Summer** by Deborah Wiles

13. Samuel's Choice by Richard Berleth

14. Safe at Home by Sharon Robinson

15. The Real Slam Dunk by Charisse K. Richardson

16. More Than Anything Else by Marie Bradby

17. Koya Delaney and the Good Girl Blues by Eloise Greenfield

18. Gloria's Way by Ann Cameron

19. Freedom Crossing by Margaret Goff Clark

20. Circle of Gold by Candy Dawson Boyd

Personal Finance

1. **Buying**

   http://www.takechargeamerica.org/wp-content/themes/tca/pdfs/teaching-resources/grade-two-buying.pdf

2. **Savings and Budget**

   http://www.takechargeamerica.org/wp-content/themes/tca/pdfs/teaching-resources/grade-two-savings-and-budget.pdf

3. **Market Prices**

   http://www.takechargeamerica.org/wp-content/themes/tca/pdfs/teaching-resources/grade-two-market-prices.pdf

4. **Managing My Money**

   http://www.takechargeamerica.org/wp-content/themes/tca/pdfs/teaching-resources/grade-two-managing-my-money.pdf

5. **Counting Change and Changing Coins**

   http://www.takechargeamerica.org/wp-content/themes/tca/pdfs/teaching-resources/grade-two-counting-change-and-changing-coins.pdf

6. **Keeping Track of Our Money**

   http://www.takechargeamerica.org/wp-content/themes/tca/pdfs/teaching-resources/grade-two-keeping-track-of-our-money.pdf

7. **Comparison Shopping**

   http://www.takechargeamerica.org/wp-content/themes/tca/pdfs/teaching-resources/grade-two-comparison-shopping.pdf

Questions To Ask **BEFORE** an IEP Meeting

1. What is the goal of this meeting?
2. Can we create an agenda for this meeting?
3. May I have a copy of my child's most recent IEP document to follow along as we talk in the meeting?
4. Can you please provide me with prior access of forms that we will be discussing during the meeting?
5. Who at the meeting will be qualified to interpret the results of my child's independent educational evaluation?

Questions To Ask **DURING** the IEP Meeting

6. How does everyone at the meeting know or work with my child?
7. Could you tell me about my child's day so I can understand what it looks like?
8. Can you explain how what you're seeing from my child is different from other kids in the classroom?
9. Could we walk through the current program and IEP plan piece by piece.
10. How is my child doing in making progress toward his IEP goals?

11. What changes in goals would the team recommend?

12. Is this a S.M.A.R.T goal? (SMART goals are Specific, Measurable, Attainable, Relevant, and Timely)

13. How is this goal measured and my child's progress monitored?

14. How will my child be assessed according to grade level?

15. Who will work on that with my child? How? When? Where and how often?

16. What training does the staff have in this specific intervention?

17. What does that accommodation/instructional intervention look like in the classroom?

18. What support will the classroom teacher have in putting these accommodations /interventions into place?

19. What can I do at home to support the IEP goals?

20. I'd like to see the final IEP before agreeing to any changes suggested at this meeting. When can I see a copy?

21. When will the changes to his program begin?

22. How will we let my child know about any program changes?

23. Can we make a plan for keeping in touch about how everything is going?

24. May I have a copy of the notes the teacher referenced during this meeting?

25. If I have questions about the information I've been given about my child's rights, who's the person to talk to for answers?

26. Who's the person to contact if I want to call another meeting?

NOTES

....

....

....

....

....

....

NOTES

_____

_____

_____

_____

_____

_____

_____

_____

NOTES

3rd Grade Curriculum

Introduction

Third grade is what Donald J. Hernandez, a professor of sociology at CUNY–Hunter College, calls a "pivot point." A study Hernandez conducted, released last year by the Annie E. Casey Foundation, found that third-graders who lack proficiency in reading are four times more likely to become high school dropouts. Several years ago the president of Wakenhut, America's largest private security company, when asked "how do you all decide how many prison beds you're going to need in the future?' He replied that they look at the number of third-graders who have to repeat third grade. Current presidential candidate Hillary Rodham Clinton stated in her Take Back American 2007 speech when she was U.S Senator stated "There are states in our country who actually plan how many prison beds they will need by looking at third-grade reading scores. They look at the failure rates and they extrapolate how many prison spots they're going to need in 10 to 15 years." So black girls and boys need to understand issues at this stage such as mass incarceration, continue to keep black boys and girls engaged in reading and writing. Also introducing your child to a mentor can have a great effect on students at this age, as well as, teaching them the structure of the family.

KEYS POINTS

- Make child read EVERDAY
- Family Structure
- Mentor

- What is Mass Incarceration?
- Continue Sex Education
- Personal Finance

Before entering the 4th grade the student should be able to:

1) Work cooperatively and productively with other children in small groups to complete projects

2) Understand how choices affect consequences

3) Become more organized and logical in their thinking processes

4) Build stronger friendships

5) Be more influenced by peer pressure because friends are very important at this stage

6) Like immediate rewards for behavior

7) Be able to copy from a chalkboard

8) Be able to write neatly in cursive because the small muscles of the hand have developed

9) Read longer stories and chapter books with expression and comprehension of the theme

10) Use prefixes, suffixes, and root words and other strategies to identify unfamiliar words

11) Multiply and divide single- and multi-digit numbers

12) Know the products of all one-digit numbers by memory

13) Tell time to the nearest quarter- and half-hour and to five minutes and one minute, using AM and PM

14) Be able to conduct week(s)-long interviews and research projects and write on a topic

15) Use linking words such as *because, therefore, since, for example, also, another, and, more*, and *but* to show sequence, contrast, and causation

16) Be prepared for a discussion, having read or studied required material

17) Recognize 3rd grade Dolch Wordlist- (50-75% of all words used in school books, library books, newspapers, and magazines are in the Dolch Basic Sight Vocabulary of 220 words (preschool thru Grade 3).

about	better	bring
carry	clean	cut
done	draw	drink
fall	far	full
got	grow	hold

hot	hurt	if
keep	kind	laugh
light	long	much
myself	never	only
own	pick	shall

show	small	start
today	together	try
warm	six	6
seven	7	10
eight	8	ten

Links for Educational Material

1) http://www.education.com

2) http://www.tlsbooks.com

3) www.kidzone.ws

4) http://www.sheppardsoftware.com

5) http://www.internet4classrooms.com

6) http://www.education.com

7) https://www.pinterest.com

8) http://www.writingprompts.net

Money Apps for Kids

- P2KMoney
- Kids Money
- Save! The Game
- Planet Orange
- Savings Quest
- Rich Kid Smart Kid
- H.I.P. Pocket Change
- PBS Kids Mad Money Game

Speech and Language Apps

- ✓ Artic Pix
- ✓ Kaufman Cards
- ✓ Speech Tutor
- ✓ Talking Tom

- ✓ WH Questions
- ✓ Conversation Builder

Math Apps

- ✓ Counting Money
- ✓ Counting Bills & Coins
- ✓ Splash Math
- ✓ Math Express
- ✓ Counting and Addition! Math and Numbers educational games by I Learn With

Family

1. **Types of Family Structures**

   http://family.lovetoknow.com/about-family-values/types-family-structures

2. **Family Structure in the United States**

   https://en.wikipedia.org/wiki/Family_structure_in_the_United_States

3. **How Slavery Affected the African American Family**

   http://nationalhumanitiescenter.org/tserve/freedom/1609-1865/essays/aafamilies.htm

3rd grade writing ideas

1. https://www.pinterest.com/vrmcguire/3rd-grade-writing-ideas/

2. https://www.teachervision.com/creative-writing/printable/54687.html

3. http://www.greatschools.org/gk/articles/third-grade-learning-games-and-activities/

4. http://www.scholastic.com/parents/resources/article/what-to-expect-grade/leap-ahead-writing-3rd-grade

How to tie a Tie

https://www.youtube.com/watch?v=utwtpwMib_A

HOW TO TIE A...
REGULAR KNOT

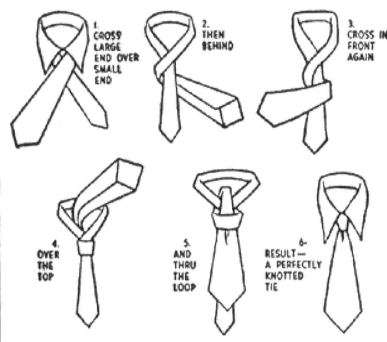

Mass Incarceration

1. **21 Facts about Mass Incarceration**

   http://www.infowars.com/mass-incarceration-21-amazing-facts-about-americas-obsession-with-prison/

2. **Facts about Mass Incarceration and Black People**

   https://afsc.org/story/facts-about-mass-incarceration-people-color-us

Sex Education Discussion Topics

- Identify basic structure of the male and female reproductive system
- Describe the function of the male and female reproductive system (menstrual cycle, nocturnal emissions)
- Explain why being yourself is important

Mentor Organizations

1. http://www.mentoring.org/
2. http://www.bbbs.org/site/c.9iILI3NGKhK6F/b.5962335/k.BE16/Home.htm
3. http://www.100blackmen.org/home.aspx
4. http://steveharveymentoring.com/camps/
5. http://www.caresmentoring.org/
6. http://girlswhoruletheworld.org/mentoring/
7. http://www.mourningfamilyfoundation.org/charities-view/honey-shine-mentoring-program/

Entrepreneurship

1. **What is an entrepreneur?**

   A. A person who organizes and operates a business or businesses, taking on greater than normal financial risks in order to do so.

   synonyms: businessman/businesswoman, enterpriser, speculator, tycoon, magnate,mogul; More

   B. a promoter in the entertainment industry.

2. **What's the difference between a Leader and a Manager?**

   http://www.forbes.com/sites/kenkrogue/2013/07/03/what-is-an-entrepreneur/

3. **5 Traits of a Good Business Leader**

   https://www.youtube.com/watch?v=8xFXTSEknbk

African American Historical Figures

1. **William Whipper: Non-Violent Business Activist-**

   http://www.aaregistry.org/historic_events/view/william-whipper-thoughtful-abolitionist

2. **William Leidesdorff: Maneuvering Millionaire-**

   http://www.blackpast.org/aaw/leidesdorff-william-alexander-1810-1848

3. **Isaac Myers: Businessman, Labor Organizer-**

   http://www.blackpast.org/aah/myers-isaac-1835-1891

4. **John Merrick: Insurance Pioneer-**

   http://www.northcarolinahistory.org/encyclopedia/379/entry/

5. **Madame C.J. Walker: Cosmetics Manufacturer-**

   http://www.biography.com/people/madam-cj-walker-9522174

6. **Maggie L Walker: Banker, Organizer-**

   http://www.encyclopediavirginia.org/Maggie_Lena_Walker_1864-1934

7. **Jesse Binga: Banker-Financier-**

   http://www.blackpast.org/aah/binga-jesse-1865-1950

8. **Anthony Overton: Banker, Manufacturer -**

   http://www.blackhistoryheroes.com/2010/02/anthony-overton-black-manufacturer.html

9. **Robert S. Abbott: The Lonely Warrior-**

   http://www.aaregistry.org/historic_events/view/robert-abbott-founder-chicago-defender

10. **Robert L. Vann: Pittsburgh Courier Founder-**

    http://en.wikipedia.org/wiki/Robert_Lee_Vann

11. **Frank L. Gillespie: Founder of the Supreme Life Insurance Co.-**

    http://www.blackhistoryheroes.com/2010/02/supreme-liberty-life-insurance-co.html

12. **C.C. Spaulding: Builder of the North Carolina Mutual Life Insurance Co.-**

    http://docsouth.unc.edu/nc/myfuture/bio.html

13. **Claude A. Barnett: Founder of the Associated Negro Press-**

    http://www.blackpast.org/aah/barnett-claude-albert-1889-1967

14. **A.G. Gaston: Millionaire, Free Enterprise-**

    http://en.wikipedia.org/wiki/A._G._Gaston

15. **John H. Johnson: Publisher Without a Peer-**

    http://www.referenceforbusiness.com/biography/F-L/Johnson-John-H-1918.html

16. **Paul R. Williams: Architect of Fame and Fortune-**

    http://en.wikipedia.org/wiki/Paul_Williams_%28architect%29

17. **Martin De Porres: A Sainted Life**

    http://www.biography.com/people/saint-mart%C3%ADn-de-porres-37827

18. **Augustus Tolton: First Negro Priest in America**

   http://www.rootsweb.ancestry.com/~momonroe/tolton.htm

19. **Richard Allen: Founder of African Methodist Episcopal Church-**

   http://www.aaregistry.org/historic_events/view/richard-allen-bishop-ames-first-leader

20. **Daniel Alexander Payne: A Giant of the A.M.E. Church**

   http://www.blackpast.org/aah/payne-daniel-alexander-1811-1893

21. **James Augustine Healy: First Negro Catholic Bishop**

   http://www.blackpast.org/aah/healy-bishop-james-augustine-1830-1900

22. **Henry McNeal Turner: Minister Extraordinaire**

   http://www.georgiaencyclopedia.org/articles/history-archaeology/henry-mcneal-turner-1834-1915

23. **John Jasper: Outstanding Slavery-Emancipation Preacher**

   http://www.blackpast.org/aah/jasper-john-j-1812-1901

24. **Adam Clayton Powell, Sr.: Builder of America's Largest Congregation**

   http://en.wikipedia.org/wiki/Adam_Clayton_Powell,_Sr.

25. **Howard Thurman: Theologian-Author**

   http://en.wikipedia.org/wiki/Howard_Thurman

African American 3rd Grade Books

1. Freedom School by Lesa Cline-Ransome

2. My Name is Truth by Ann Turner

3. Brown Girl Dreaming by Jacqueline Woodson

4. Firebird by Misty Copeland

5. The Blossoming Universe of Violet Diamond by Brenda Woods

6. The Perfect Place by Teresa E. Harris

7. Africa Is My Home: A Child of the Amistad by Monica Edinger

8. Hold Fast by Blue Balliett

9. Nelson Mandela by Kadir Nelson

10. .Sugar by Jewell Parker Rhodes

Personal Finance

1. **Debt**

   http://www.takechargeamerica.org/wp-content/themes/tca/pdfs/teaching-resources/grade-three-debt.pdf

2. **Saving**

   http://www.takechargeamerica.org/wp-content/themes/tca/pdfs/teaching-resources/grade-three-saving.pdf

3. **Labor, Choice, Sales Tax**

   http://www.takechargeamerica.org/wp-content/themes/tca/pdfs/teaching-resources/grade-three-labor-choice-sales-tax.pdf

4. **Savings Plan**

   http://www.takechargeamerica.org/wp-content/themes/tca/pdfs/teaching-resources/grade-three-savings-plan.pdf

5. **I Want it All**

   http://www.takechargeamerica.org/wp-content/themes/tca/pdfs/teaching-resources/grade-three-i-want-it-all.pdf

6. **Coupon Clippers**

   http://www.takechargeamerica.org/wp-content/themes/tca/pdfs/teaching-resources/grade-three-coupon-clippers.pdf

7. **Shopping Smarter**

   http://www.takechargeamerica.org/wp-content/themes/tca/pdfs/teaching-resources/grade-three-shopping-smarter.pdf

8. **Wealth**

   http://www.takechargeamerica.org/wp-content/themes/tca/pdfs/teaching-resources/grade-three-wealth.pdf

9. **Mental Money**

   http://www.takechargeamerica.org/wp-content/themes/tca/pdfs/teaching-resources/grade-three-mental-money.pdf

NOTES

....

....

....

....

....

....

NOTES

_____

_____

_____

_____

_____

_____

_____

_____

NOTES

4th Grade Curriculum

Introduction

Fourth graders typically face new challenges and their increasing awareness of others and the world around them can be unnerving. Hair twisting, stomachaches, and headaches are common manifestations of the tension and anxiety that are common at this age. Industrious and curious, they are often ready and eager for new knowledge. Fourth graders begin to gather information independently but yet they are still concrete thinkers and need to learn by application: creating posters, putting on plays, writing stories, reading books, playing games, and using math manipulatives to support abstract math concepts. Kids are going to listen to music so it's best that we build on that passion and use it as a tool for teaching. Former President Barack Obama had Jay-Z on his iPod and with hip hop being such a large part of African American youth culture, as parents you can integrate that in writing topics or discuss the pedagogy of music or hip hop with your child.

KEYS POINTS

- Make child read EVERDAY
- Pedagogy of Hip Hop
- Mentor
- What is Prison Industrial Complex?
- Personal Finance
- Links of young entrepreneurs

Before entering the 5ᵗʰ grade the student should be able to:

1)   Begin to make more decisions and engage in group decision-making

2)   Want to be part of a group

3)   Think independently and critically

4)   Have empathy

5)   Show a strong sense of responsibility

6)   Have a greater awareness of fairness

7)   Be able to memorize and recite facts, although he may not have a deep understanding of them

8)   Increase the amount of detail in drawings

9)   Work on research projects

10) Write a structured paragraph with an introductory topic sentence, three supporting details, and a closing sentence that wraps up the main idea of the paragraph

11) Use quotations effectively in writing

12) Use a range of strategies when drawing meaning from text, such as prediction, connections, and inference

13) Correct frequently misused words (e.g. *too, to, two; their, they're, there*)

14) Understand more complex cause-and-effect relationships

15) Add and subtract decimals, and compare decimals and fractions

16) Multiply multi-digit numbers by two-digit numbers, understanding the concept of place value

17) Divide larger multi-digit numbers by one-digit numbers, understanding the concept of place value

18) Identify points, lines, rays, and angles in two-dimensional figures

Links for Educational Material

1.   http://www.education.com

2.   http://www.tlsbooks.com

3.   www.kidzone.ws

4.   http://www.sheppardsoftware.com

5. http://www.internet4classrooms.com

6. http://www.education.com

7. https://www.pinterest.com/abbiebart3/

8. http://www.abcya.com/fourth_grade_computers.htm

Money Apps for Kids

- P2KMoney
- Kids Money
- Save! The Game
- Planet Orange
- Savings Quest
- Rich Kid Smart Kid
- H.I.P. Pocket Change
- PBS Kids Mad Money Game

Math Apps

- ✓ Counting Money
- ✓ Counting Bills & Coins
- ✓ Splash Math
- ✓ Math Express
- ✓ Counting and Addition! Math and Numbers educational games by i Learn With

Prison Industrial Complex

1. **What is the Prison Industrial Complex?**

The prison industrial complex (PIC) is a term we use to describe the overlapping interests of government and industry that use surveillance, policing, and imprisonment as solutions to economic, social and political problems.

2. **Who's getting rich off the Prison Industrial Complex**

http://www.vice.com/read/whos-getting-rich-off-the-prison-industrial-complex

3. **Shocking Facts about Americas for Profit Prison**

http://www.truth-out.org/news/item/21694-shocking-facts-about-americas-for-profit-prison-industry#

4. **Angela Davis: Slavery and the Prison Industrial Complex**

https://www.youtube.com/watch?v=BasNj57GvTA

5. **Michelle Alexander on The New Jim Crow: Mass Incarceration in the Age of Colorblindness**

   https://www.youtube.com/watch?v=k9FSBUv6uyI

4th grade writing ideas

1. **Writing Prompts**

   http://www.internet4classrooms.com/grade_level_help/writing_prompt_language_arts_fourth_4th_grade.htm

2. **Expository Writing Prompts**

   http://expositorywritingprompts.com/4th-grade-writing-prompts/

3. **73 Exciting Journal Starters**

   http://journalbuddies.com/journal_prompts__journal_topics/4th-grade-writing-prompts-73-exciting-journal-starters-for-kids/

What is an HBCU?

A college or university that was originally founded to educate students of African-American descent.

About HBCU's

https://www.thurgoodmarshallfund.net/about-tmcf/about-hbcus

The Importance of HBCUs and the Family

http://www.aces.edu/urban/metronews/vol6no1/HBCUs.html

Pedagogy of Hip Hop

1. **Dr. Diop and DJ Que Yi present Hip Hop in the Classroom**

   https://www.youtube.com/watch?v=xqBMlAKMlTg

2. **Marc Lamont Hill on Using Hip Hop in the Classroom**

   https://www.youtube.com/watch?v=ZKf0EnhWL-I

3. **Hip Hop, Pedagogy & Race Within the Classroom**

   https://www.youtube.com/watch?v=BfP_IFlL74A

Mentor Organizations

1. http://www.mentoring.org/
2. http://www.bbbs.org/site/c.9iILI3NGKhK6F/b.5962335/k.BE16/Home.htm
3. http://www.100blackmen.org/home.aspx
4. http://steveharveymentoring.com/camps/
5. http://www.caresmentoring.org/
6. http://girlswhoruletheworld.org/mentoring/
7. http://www.mourningfamilyfoundation.org/charities-view/honey-shine-mentoring-program/

Young Entrepreneurs

1. **Young Black Entrepreneurs**

   https://www.youtube.com/watch?v=zhl9gsgzcrk

2. **11 year old Ceo of Mo's Bow's**

   https://www.youtube.com/watch?v=jTRMV64uKGk

3. **Jaylen Bledsoe worth $3.5 million dollars**

   https://www.youtube.com/watch?v=ybOEe-AxJV8

4. **Maya Penn**

   https://www.youtube.com/watch?v=BbCzizSI8mo

5. **The Super Business Girl. The 11 Year Old CEO**

   https://www.youtube.com/watch?v=VdQcFn-842s

African American Historical Figures

1. **Ira Aldridge: Black Tragedian**

   http://www.blackpast.org/aah/aldridge-ira-1807-1867

2. **Charles Gilpin: Pioneer Dramatic Actor**

   http://en.wikipedia.org/wiki/Charles_Sidney_Gilpin

3. **Bert Williams: A Comedian's Comedian**

   http://www.notablebiographies.com/supp/Supplement-Sp-Z/Williams-Bert.html

4. **Richard B. Harrison: The Original "De Lawd"**

http://www.blackpast.org/aah/harrison-richard-b-1864-1935

5. **Frank Silvera: An "Everyman" of the Theatre**

http://en.wikipedia.org/wiki/Frank_Silvera

6. **Canada Lee: "Bigger Thomas"**

http://en.wikipedia.org/wiki/Canada_Lee

7. **Ethel Waters: Thirty Years on Stage**

http://www.biography.com/people/ethel-waters-9524982

8. **Katherine Dunham: With Roots in Rhythm and Race**

http://kdcah.org/katherine-dunham-biography/

9. **Sidney Poitier: Oscar-Winning Dramatic Star**

http://www.biography.com/people/sidney-poitier-9443345

10. **George P. Bridgetower: Composer**

http://en.wikipedia.org/wiki/George_Bridgetower

11. **Samuel Coleridge-Taylor: English Composer**

http://en.wikipedia.org/wiki/Samuel_Coleridge-Taylor

12. **James Bland: Composer of Southern Songs**

http://www.blackpast.org/aah/bland-james-1854-1911

13. **Blind Lemon Jefferson: Best of the Blues Bards-**

http://www.biography.com/people/blind-lemon-jefferson-41017

14. **Harry T. Burleigh: Singer, Composer, Arranger**

http://en.wikipedia.org/wiki/Harry_Burleigh

15. **Nathaniel Dett: Composer**

http://en.wikipedia.org/wiki/Robert_Nathaniel_Dett

16. **W.C. Handy: "The Father of the Blues"**

http://www.biography.com/people/wc-handy-39700

17. William Grant Still: Modern Composer

http://en.wikipedia.org/wiki/William_Grant_Still

18. William L. Dawson: Composer-Arranger

http://en.wikipedia.org/wiki/William_L._Dawson_%28composer%29

19. Paul Robeson: A Baritone To Remember

http://www.cpsr.cs.uchicago.edu/robeson/bio.html

20. Roland Hayes: God's Own Tenor

http://en.wikipedia.org/wiki/Roland_Hayes

21. Dean Dixon: Conductor International

http://www.blackpast.org/aah/dixon-charles-dean-1915-1976

22. Louis "Satchmo" Armstrong: The Jazz Ambassador

http://www.biography.com/people/louis-armstrong-9188912

23. Duke Ellington: The Maestro

http://www.biography.com/people/duke-ellington-9286338

24. Marian Anderson: This Century's Contralto

http://www.notablebiographies.com/A-An/Anderson-Marian.html

25. Ulysses Kay: In a Classical Vein

http://en.wikipedia.org/wiki/Ulysses_Kay

African American 4th Grade Books

1. When the Beat Was Born: DJ Cool Herc and the Creation of Hip Hop by Laban Carrick Hill

2. Ellen's Broom by Kelly Starling Lyons

3. Spirit Seeker: John Coltrane's Musical Journey by Gary Golio

4. The Lion's of Little Rock by Kristin Levine

5. What Color is my world?: The Lost history of African American Inventors by Kareem Abdul-Jabbar and Raymond Obstfeld

6. Around Our Way On Neighbors' Day by Tameka Fryer Brown

7. Ben and the Emancipation Proclamation by Pat Sherman

8. Dave the Potter: Artist, Poet, Slave by Laban Carrick Hill

9. .Ruth and the Green Book by Calvin Alexander Ramsey

10. Finding Lincoln by Ann Malaspina

Personal Finance

1. **Characteristics and functions of Money**

    http://www.takechargeamerica.org/wp-content/themes/tca/pdfs/teaching-resources/grade-four-characteristics-and-functions-of-money.pdf

2. **Role of Money**

    http://www.takechargeamerica.org/wp-content/themes/tca/pdfs/teaching-resources/grade-four-the-role-of-money.pdf

3. **Spending Money**

    http://www.takechargeamerica.org/wp-content/themes/tca/pdfs/teaching-resources/grade-four-spending-money.pdf

4. **Savings and Earnings**

    http://www.takechargeamerica.org/wp-content/themes/tca/pdfs/teaching-resources/grade-four-savings-and-earnings.pdf

5. **Earning an Income**

    http://www.takechargeamerica.org/wp-content/themes/tca/pdfs/teaching-resources/grade-four-earning-an-income.pdf

6. **Borrowing and Lending**

    http://www.takechargeamerica.org/wp-content/themes/tca/pdfs/teaching-resources/grade-four-borrowing-and-lending.pdf

7. **What's the Price**

    http://www.takechargeamerica.org/wp-content/themes/tca/pdfs/teaching-resources/grade-four-whats-the-price.pdf

8. **Using Credit and Spending Money Wisely**

    http://www.takechargeamerica.org/wp-content/themes/tca/pdfs/teaching-resources/grade-four-using-credit-and-spending-money-wisely.pdf

9. **Do you really need it?**

    http://www.takechargeamerica.org/wp-content/themes/tca/pdfs/teaching-resources/grade-four-do-you-really-need-it.pdf

10. **Taxes**

    http://www.takechargeamerica.org/wp-content/themes/tca/pdfs/teaching-resources/grade-four-taxes.pdf

NOTES

....

....

....

....

....

....

....

....

....

....

....

NOTES

NOTES

5th Grade Curriculum

Introduction

In the fifth grade your child has finally become comfortable in elementary school. They will learn to read text fluently with good comprehension and write with organization. At this stage it's crucial that your child improves their higher order thinking skills and learns how to understand and process complex events. In this section they will learn how the reconstruction affected African Americans, what "Black Wall Street" was about and what it means to be financially free. This is also the stage when they should become active with the internet by not just looking at videos on it but actually creating a YouTube video and channel.

KEYS POINTS

- Make child read EVERDAY
- How to Make a YouTube Video
- Black Wall Street
- The Reconstruction
- Financial Freedom
- How to tie a Bowtie

Before entering the 6th grade the student should be able to:

1) Be generally truthful and dependable

2) Develop increasing independence

3) Improve problem-solving skills

4) Acquire increasingly advanced listening and responding skills, such as responding to peers' comments and opinions

5) Enjoy organizing and classifying objects and ideas

6) Be able to read and concentrate for long periods of time

7) Read complex text fluently and with good comprehension

8) Research a topic using a variety of sources, and use the features of a book (for example, the index, glossary, and appendix) to find information

9) Identify conflict, climax, and resolution in a story

10) Write an organized, multi-paragraph composition in sequential order with a central idea

11) Correctly use commas and quotation marks in writing

12) Use problem-solving strategies to solve real-world math problems

13) Add and subtract fractions and decimals

14) Understand and do math problems involving parentheses, brackets, and braces

15) Classify two dimensional figures into different categories (e.g. a rectangle has four right angles, so a square is always a rectangle)

16) Find the area of two-dimensional shapes

17) Use long division to divide large numbers by multi-digit numbers

18) Identify and map a pair of coordinate numbers on the coordinate system (along the x-axis and y-axis)

Links for Educational Material

1. http://www.education.com

2. http://www.tlsbooks.com

3. www.kidzone.ws

4. http://www.sheppardsoftware.com

5. http://www.internet4classrooms.com

6. https://www.time4learning.com/scope-sequence/5th_grade_science.shtml

7. http://everydaymath.uchicago.edu/parents/5th-grade/em-at-home/

8. https://www.ixl.com/math/grade-5

9. http://www.education.com/activity/fifth-grade/science/

Money Apps for Kids

- P2KMoney
- Kids Money
- Save! The Game
- Planet Orange
- Savings Quest
- Rich Kid Smart Kid
- H.I.P. Pocket Change
- PBS Kids Mad Money Game

Black Wall Street

1. **Black Wall Street**

   https://en.wikipedia.org/wiki/The_Black_Wall_Street

2. **The Night Tulsa Burned**

   https://www.youtube.com/watch?v=yLwVxyD7A98

3. **Black Wall Street: The Hidden American Holocaust**

   https://www.youtube.com/watch?v=jBmauP_X5DI

5th grade writing ideas

1. **Writing Prompts**

   http://www.writingprompts.net/5th-grade/

2. **Writers Notebook Prompts**

   https://www.pinterest.com/celewi05/5th-grade-writing-writers-notebook-prompts/

3. **72 Writing Ideas**

   http://journalbuddies.com/journal_prompts__journal_topics/5th-grade-writing-prompts-seventy-two-writing-ideas-for-kids/

How to Make a YouTube video

1. **HOW TO MAKE VIDEOS AND START A YOUTUBE CHANNEL**

   https://www.youtube.com/watch?v=bgndSmYPO78

2. **How to Start a YouTube Channel**

   https://www.youtube.com/watch?v=mRbiMtDdQXs

3. **How To Make Your 1st YouTube Video With Powerpoint**

https://www.youtube.com/watch?v=XiQr5efiW7o

The Reconstruction

1. **Reconstruction and Its Aftermath**

http://memory.loc.gov/ammem/aaohtml/exhibit/aopart5.html

2. **Effects of Reconstruction**

https://www.youtube.com/watch?v=P92hENQ2fCA

Mentor Organizations

1. http://www.mentoring.org/
2. http://www.bbbs.org/site/c.9iILI3NGKhK6F/b.5962335/k.BE16/Home.htm
3. http://www.100blackmen.org/home.aspx
4. http://steveharveymentoring.com/camps/
5. http://www.caresmentoring.org/
6. http://girlswhoruletheworld.org/mentoring/
7. http://www.mourningfamilyfoundation.org/charities-view/honey-shine-mentoring-program/

How to tie a Bowtie

https://www.youtube.com/watch?v=AEjF-MzzqaE

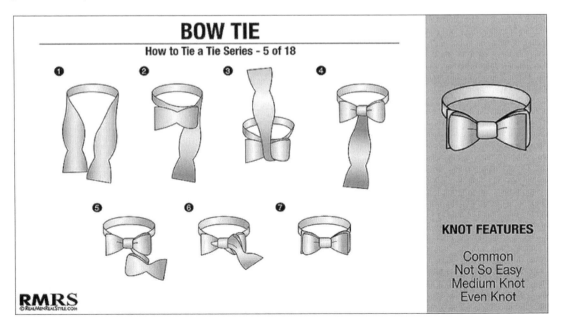

7 Stages to Small Business Success

1. http://smallbiztrends.com/2013/02/small-business-success-seven-stages.html
2. http://www.forbes.com/sites/stevenberglas/2012/09/20/seven-7-steps-to-entrepreneurial-success/

Financial Freedom

1. **5 Steps to Understanding Financial Freedom**

   https://www.youtube.com/watch?v=GizFdgX8jJM

2. **My grandmother was a financial genius**

   https://www.youtube.com/watch?v=tF_KoJUM3Cw

African American Historical Figures

1. **Leontyne Price: Prima Donna** http://www.biography.com/people/leontyne-price-9446930

2. **Robert Duncanson: Early American Artist** http://blackhistorynow.com/robert-s-duncanson/

3. **Edward M. Bannister: Landscape Painter**

   http://en.wikipedia.org/wiki/Edward_Mitchell_Bannister

4. **Henry Ossawa Tanner: A Painter of Religious Subjects**

   http://en.wikipedia.org/wiki/Henry_Ossawa_Tanner

5. **Edmonia Lewis: Pioneer Woman Sculptor**

   http://en.wikipedia.org/wiki/Edmonia_Lewis

6. **Horace Pippen: Modern Primitive** http://www.biography.com/people/horace-pippin-9441456

7. **Malvin Gray Johnson: Symbolic Abstractionist**

   http://en.wikipedia.org/wiki/Malvin_Gray_Johnson

8. **Richmond Barthe: Realistic Sculptor** http://www.blackpast.org/aah/barthe-richmond-1901-1988

9. **Jacob Lawrence: Painter, Contemporary Primitive**

   http://www.biography.com/people/jacob-lawrence-9375562

10. **Marion Perkins: Sculptor**

    http://www.encyclopedia.com/doc/1G2-2874000053.html

11. **Charles Alston: Famed Muralist** http://www.thefamouspeople.com/profiles/charles-alston-356.php

12. **Geraldine McCullough: Painter-Sculptor**

    http://www.thehistorymakers.com/biography/geraldine-mccullough-39

13. **E. Simms Campbell: Cartoonist** http://www.biography.com/people/e-simms-campbell-37932

14. **Gordon Roger Parks: Master of the Camera**

    http://www.biography.com/people/gordon-parks-37379

15. **Malcolm X**

    http://www.biography.com/people/malcolm-x-9396195

16. **James Meredith**

    http://www.biography.com/people/james-meredith-9406314

17. **Elijah Muhammad**

    http://www.biography.com/people/elijah-muhammad-9417458#synopsis

18. **Rosa Parks**

    http://www.biography.com/people/rosa-parks-9433715

19. **Bobby Seale**

    http://www.biography.com/people/bobby-seale-9477529

20. **Fred Shuttlesworth**

    http://www.biography.com/news/fred-shuttlesworth-alabama-civil-rights-black-history-video

21. **Emmett Till**

    http://www.biography.com/people/emmett-till-507515

22. **Ida Bell Wells-Barnett**

    http://www.biography.com/people/ida-b-wells-9527635

23. **Walter White**

    http://www.biography.com/people/walter-white-9529708

24. **Roy Wilkins**

   http://www.biography.com/people/roy-wilkins-9531564

25. **Josephine Baker**

   http://www.biography.com/people/josephine-baker-9195959

African American 5th Grade Books

1. Let Freedom Sing by Vanessa Newton

2. Make Way for Dyamonde Daniel by Nikki Grimes

3. Marching for Freedom: Walk Together Children and Don't You Grow Wear by Elizabeth Partridge

4. Peace, Locomotion by Jacqueline Woodson

5. Ron's Big Mission by Rose Blue and Corianne J. Naden

6. The Listeners by Gloria Whelan

7. I Get So Hungry by Bebe Moore Campbell

8. Elijah of Buxton by Christopher Paul Curtis

9. One Million Men and Me by Kelly Starling Lyons

10. All of the Above by Shelley Pearsall

Personal Finance

1. **Production and Trade**

   http://www.takechargeamerica.org/wp-content/themes/tca/pdfs/teaching-resources/grade-five-production-and-trade.pdf

2. **Starting your own Business**

   http://www.takechargeamerica.org/wp-content/themes/tca/pdfs/teaching-resources/grade-five-starting-your-own-business.pdf

3. **Government Goods and Services**

   http://www.takechargeamerica.org/wp-content/themes/tca/pdfs/teaching-resources/grade-five-government-goods-and-services.pdf

4. **Wise Shoppers**

   http://www.takechargeamerica.org/wp-content/themes/tca/pdfs/teaching-resources/grade-five-wise-shoppers.pdf

5. **Saving and creating a personal budget**

    http://www.takechargeamerica.org/wp-content/themes/tca/pdfs/teaching-resources/grade-five-saving-and-creating-a-personal-budget.pdf

6. **Saving and Investing**

    http://www.takechargeamerica.org/wp-content/themes/tca/pdfs/teaching-resources/grade-five-saving-and-investing.pdf

7. **Using Credit**

    http://www.takechargeamerica.org/wp-content/themes/tca/pdfs/teaching-resources/grade-five-using-credit.pdf

8. **Short term and long term savings goals**

    http://www.takechargeamerica.org/wp-content/themes/tca/pdfs/teaching-resources/grade-five-short-term-and-long-term-savings-goals.pdf

9. **Currency and Exchange Rates**

    http://www.takechargeamerica.org/wp-content/themes/tca/pdfs/teaching-resources/grade-five-currency-and-exchange-rates.pdf

10. **How do you spend your money**

    http://www.takechargeamerica.org/wp-content/themes/tca/pdfs/teaching-resources/grade-five-how-do-you-spend-your-money.pdf

NOTES

....

....

....

....

....

....

NOTES

_____

_____

_____

_____

_____

_____

_____

_____

6th Grade Curriculum

Introduction

Many education consultants whom are deeply passionate about preparing and guiding the next generation of leaders worldwide believe that students should begin preparing for college in the sixth grade. They are all in agreement that students need time to fully develop and unleash their maximum potential. This increases the student's opportunities dramatically to receive scholarships as well as acceptance in various universities. This section includes the various parts of a business, reparations; how to create a successful blog, how crack cocaine entered the black and brown neighborhoods and shedding some light on how difficult it is to become a professional athlete.

KEYS POINTS

- Iran-Contra Scandal
- Parts of a Business Plan
- Reparations
- How to create a blog
- Debunking the Athlete

Before entering the 7th grade the student should be able to:

1) Express concerns directly
2) Stand up for a friend
3) Experience a range and intensity of emotions
4) Take on greater responsibility for her behavior and decisions

5) Possibly experience the onset of puberty

6) Analyze how authors use dialogue, imagery and mood, to develop the plot, characters, point of view, and theme in literature

7) Read, retell and summarize grade-level appropriate narrative and informational texts

8) Write a multi-paragraph composition with writing strategies such as dialogue and suspense

9) Define good writing by others and identify the strengths and weaknesses in his own writing

10) Begin taking simple notes

11) Multiply and divide common fractions and mixed numbers

12) Perform multi-step math word problems

Links for Educational Material

1. http://www.funbrain.com/FBSearch.php?Grade=6

2. http://www.education.com

3. http://www.tlsbooks.com

4. www.kidzone.ws

5. http://www.sheppardsoftware.com

6. http://www.internet4classrooms.com

7. http://www.education.com

Money Apps for Kids

- P2KMoney
- Kids Money
- Save! The Game
- Planet Orange
- Savings Quest
- Rich Kid Smart Kid
- H.I.P. Pocket Change
- PBS Kids Mad Money Game

Math Apps

- ✓ Maya Numbers
- ✓ Buzz Math
- ✓ iTooch Middle School App
- ✓ Counting and Addition! Math and Numbers educational games by i Learn With

Iran-Contra Scandal

1. **Iran-Contra Affair Scandal Explained: US History Review**

   https://www.youtube.com/watch?v=Nix_vj2DaqQ

2. **The CIA and Crack Cocaine**

   https://www.youtube.com/watch?v=lyLJtkxPC6I

3. **How Crack Funded a CIA War: Gary Webb Interview on the Contras and Ronald Reagan (1996)**

   https://www.youtube.com/watch?v=WMbEhP2irDM

6th grade writing ideas

1. **Writing Prompts**

   http://www.writingprompts.net/6th-grade/

2. **Writing Ideas**

   https://www.pinterest.com/writeaboutthis/6th-grade-writing-ideas/

3. **37 Writing Prompts**

   http://journalbuddies.com/journal_prompts__journal_topics/37-6th-grade-writing-prompts/

How to Create a Blog

1. **Make a Successful Blog ! 4 Simple Successful Blogging Tips**

   https://www.youtube.com/watch?v=vjvJRk_at-8

2. **How to start a Blog - Beginners Guide**

   https://www.youtube.com/watch?v=2y0IAhqtsjw

Reparations

Reparation for slavery is the idea that some form of compensatory payment should be made to the descendants of Africans who had been enslaved by the Atlantic Slave Trade.

3. **Facing the Truth: The Case for Reparations**

   https://www.youtube.com/watch?v=Pm9DJuTrO8Q

4. **Dr Umar On Reparations**

   https://www.youtube.com/watch?v=fNvb4-aa1vY

Parts of a Business Plan

- Executive Summary
- Company Description
- Market Analysis
- Organization & Management
- Service or Product Line
- Marketing & Sales
- Funding Request
- Financial Projections
- Appendix
- How to Make Your Business Plan Stand Out

Elements of a Business Plan

http://www.entrepreneur.com/article/38308

Debunking the Athlete Myth

1. **The Statistical Breakdown Of Becoming A Professional Athlete**

   http://elitedaily.com/sports/odds-going-pro-sports-will-make-rethink-day-job/

2. **Here Are The Odds That Your Kid Becomes A Professional Athlete**

   http://www.businessinsider.com/odds-college-athletes-become-professionals-2012-2

3. **Jalen Rose: How athletes go broke**

   https://www.youtube.com/watch?v=-362OfeM9OQ

4. **How Antoine Walker Lost NBA Riches**

   https://www.youtube.com/watch?v=APaLlppTT04

5. **Broke**

   https://www.youtube.com/watch?v=TSOAwNSv8EM

African American Historical Figures

1. **Fred Shuttlesworth**

   http://www.biography.com/news/fred-shuttlesworth-alabama-civil-rights-black-history-video

2. **Emmett Till**

   http://www.biography.com/people/emmett-till-507515

3. **Ida Bell Wells-Barnett**

   http://www.biography.com/people/ida-b-wells-9527635

4. **Walter White**

   http://www.biography.com/people/walter-white-9529708

5. **Roy Wilkins**

   http://www.biography.com/people/roy-wilkins-9531564

6. **Josephine Baker**

   http://www.biography.com/people/josephine-baker-9195959

7. **Sammy Davis Jr**

   http://www.biography.com/people/sammy-davis-jr-9268223

8. **Morgan Freeman**

   http://www.biography.com/people/morgan-freeman-9301982

9. **Gregory Hines**

   http://www.biography.com/people/gregory-hines-9542572

10. **Lena Horne**

    http://www.biography.com/people/lena-horne-9344086

11. **James Earl Jones**

    http://www.biography.com/people/james-earl-jones-9357354

12. **Spike Lee**

http://www.biography.com/people/spike-lee-9377207

13. **Eddie Murphy**

http://www.biography.com/people/eddie-murphy-9418676

14. **Richard Pryor**

http://www.biography.com/people/richard-pryor-9448082

15. **Will Smith**

http://www.biography.com/people/will-smith-9542165

16. **Denzel Washington**

http://www.biography.com/people/denzel-washington-9524687

17. **Archibald Alphonso Alexander**

http://www.blackpast.org/aah/alexander-archie-alphonso-1888-1958

18. **Patricia Bath**

http://www.biography.com/people/patricia-bath-21038525#synopsis

19. **David Crosthwalt Jr**

http://www.biography.com/people/david-nelson-crosthwait-jr-205623

20. **Mark Dean**

http://www.biography.com/people/mark-dean-604036

21. **Percy Lavon Julian**

http://www.biography.com/people/percy-julian-9359018

22. **Frederick McKinley Jones**

http://www.biography.com/people/frederick-jones-21329957#synopsis

23. **Earnest Everett Just**

http://www.biography.com/people/ernest-everett-just-9359195

24. **Mary McLeod Bethune**

http://www.biography.com/people/mary-mcleod-bethune-9211266#synopsis

25. **Garrett Augustus Morgan**

http://www.biography.com/people/garrett-morgan-9414691#synopsis

Must Watch Black Educational Films

1. Tuskegee Airman
2. Roots
3. 12 Years a Slave
4. Hidden Colors I
5. Hidden Colors II
6. The Great Debaters
7. Greatest Black Emancipation: The Haitian Revolution
8. Malcolm X
9. PBS Egalite for ALL:Toussaint Louverture and the Haitian Revolution
10. The Central Park Five

NOTES

....

....

....

....

....

....

....

....

....

....

....

....

....

....

....

....

NOTES

_____

_____

_____

_____

_____

_____

_____

NOTES

7ᵗʰ Grade Curriculum

Introduction

Seventh grade is a big change socially for students as many try to hang with the "cool" crowd and want to be popular. As a parent you must continue to talk to your child about just being themselves and not too mimic or imitate anyone else. Typically what happens when kids begin to try and "fit in" they are so focused on the social aspect that they begin to let their grades slip in the process. So we must keep them focused and eyes on the bigger picture and continue to shoot for the stars. In this section we teach your child how to write a business plan, and introduce them to billionaire entrepreneurs.

KEYS POINTS

- How to write a Business Plan
- How to create a Website
- 7 Stages to Small Business Success
- How to write a scholarship essay
- Billionaire Entrepreneurs

Before entering the 8ᵗʰ grade the student should be able to:

1) Develop complex writing skills

2) Constructively critique their own and other's writing

3) Apply punctuation, grammar, and syntax skills

4) Recognize and apply grade appropriate vocabulary

5) Read with fluency, with focus on comprehension

6) Have a solid understanding of algebraic principles

7) Be able to graph and solve linear equations

8) Understand and apply basic concepts of geometry

9) Be able to apply math to everyday activities

Entrepreneurs

1. **Mark Cuban: How I Became a Billionaire**

    https://www.youtube.com/watch?v=vrl5PFB35Ec

2. **Mark Zuckerberg: Building the Facebook Empire**

    https://www.youtube.com/watch?v=5WiDIhIkPoM

3. **Black man sells his app for a billion dollars**

    https://www.youtube.com/watch?v=ajdY9s5LAgU

Must Watch Black Films

1. Hidden Colors III

2. Hidden Colors IV

3. Have You Heard From Johannesburg?

4. 500 Years Later

5. Good Hair

6. Life and Debt

7. Cuba, An African Odyssey

8. Black In Latin America

9. The FBI's War on Black America

10. When Black Men Ruled The World

How to write a Scholarship Essay

1. **How to Write a Winning Scholarship Essay**

    http://www.supercollege.com/guide/guide.cfm?t_id=2&g_id=21&step=1

2. **4 ways to make your scholarship essay stand out**

   http://www.usnews.com/education/blogs/the-scholarship-coach/2013/01/31/4-ways-to-make-your-scholarship-essay-stand-out

3. **Writing a Winning Essay**

   https://www.youtube.com/watch?v=dA7qgEU9jnQ

7th grade writing ideas

1. **Writing Prompts**

   http://www.writingprompts.net/7th-grade/

2. **7th grade writing on Pinterest**

   https://www.pinterest.com/explore/7th-grade-writing/

3. **7th grade persuasive writing**

   https://learnzillion.com/lessonsets/369-7th-grade-persuasive-writing-responding-to-a-prompt

How to Create a Website

1. **How to Create a Business Website with WordPress - Tutorial for Beginners 2015**

   https://www.youtube.com/watch?v=orpqn-m1JpQ

2. **How to Create a Website with WordPress**

   https://www.youtube.com/watch?v=zoQ5J9RwyWw

7 Stages to Small Business Success

   http://smallbiztrends.com/2013/02/small-business-success-seven-stages.html
   http://www.forbes.com/sites/stevenberglas/2012/09/20/seven-7-steps-to-entrepreneurial-success/

African American Historical Figures

1. **Charles Henry Turner**

   http://www.biography.com/people/charles-henry-turner-21302547

2. **Ralph Bunche**

   http://www.biography.com/people/ralph-bunche-9231128#synopsis

3. **Minnie Joycelyn Elders**

http://www.biography.com/people/m-joycelyn-elders-9285785

4. **Jesse Jackson**

http://www.biography.com/people/jesse-jackson-9351181

5. **Daniel "Chappie" James**

http://www.biography.com/people/daniel-james-jr-9352497

6. **Thurgood Marshall**

http://www.biography.com/people/thurgood-marshall-9400241

7. **Kwesi Mfume**

http://www.biography.com/people/kweisi-mfume-12782299

8. **Clarence Thomas**

http://www.biography.com/people/clarence-thomas-9505658

9. **Coleman Young**

http://www.biography.com/people/coleman-young-39987

10. **Louis Armstrong**

http://www.biography.com/people/louis-armstrong-9188912

11. **Harry Belafonte**

http://www.biography.com/people/harry-belafonte-12103211

12. **Chuck Berry**

http://www.biography.com/people/chuck-berry-9210488

13. **Ray Charles**

http://www.biography.com/people/ray-charles-9245001

14. **Miles Davis**

http://www.biography.com/people/miles-davis-9267992

15. **Duke Ellington**

http://www.biography.com/people/duke-ellington-9286338

16. **Aretha Franklin**

http://www.biography.com/people/aretha-franklin-9301157

17. Dizzy Gillespie

http://www.biography.com/people/dizzy-gillespie-9311417

18. Jimi Hendrix

http://www.biography.com/people/jimi-hendrix-9334756

19. Billie Holiday

http://www.biography.com/people/billie-holiday-9341902

20. Michael Jackson

http://www.biography.com/people/michael-jackson-38211

21. Diana Ross

http://www.biography.com/people/diana-ross-9464240

22. Stevie Wonder

http://www.biography.com/people/stevie-wonder-9536078

NOTES

....

....

....

....

....

....

....

....

....

....

....

....

....

....

....

....

NOTES

NOTES

8th Grade Curriculum

Introduction

In this section we replace the educational links with free ACT and SAT testing preparation material. We need to get our black boys and girls to begin thinking at this grade about scoring exceptionally well on these college admissions test so they can compete with their classmates for various scholarships. Don't expect your child to do very well on these practice tests at this stage but they should focus on getting familiar with the questions being asked. Once they become accustomed to the questions then they will begin to build confidence that they can do well on the test and begin to focus on the things that they need to work on. We also teach them in this section how to write a scholarly article and how to write a successful college admission essay.

KEYS POINTS

- What is a "Brand"
- College Admission Essay
- Business Plan
- Freedman's Bank
- How to write a scholarly article

Before entering the 9th grade the student should be able to:

1) Develop age appropriate writing skills

2) Accurately apply punctuation, grammar, and syntax skills

3) Develop complex grade appropriate vocabulary

4) Read with fluency while applying comprehension strategies

5) Accurately apply ratio, proportion, and percent

6) Have a solid understanding of algebraic principles

7) Understand beginning concepts of geometry

8) Be able to apply data and statistics to everyday situations

ACT Preparation Material

1. https://www.number2.com/

2. http://www.4tests.com/act

3. http://www.princetonreview.com/college/free-act-practice-test#!practice

4. http://www.actstudent.org/sampletest/

5. http://www.sparknotes.com/testprep/books/act/

What is a "Brand"

1. **Branding**

   http://www.entrepreneur.com/encyclopedia/branding

2. **What is a Brand, Anyway?**

   http://www.forbes.com/sites/jerrymclaughlin/2011/12/21/what-is-a-brand-anyway/

3. **What is Branding and How Important is it to Your Marketing Strategy?**

   http://marketing.about.com/cs/brandmktg/a/whatisbranding.htm

How to write a Business Plan

1. http://www.entrepreneur.com/businessplan/index.html

2. https://www.sba.gov/writing-business-plan

3. https://www.youtube.com/watch?v=PDWvcsTloJo

Current Notable Scholars

1. **Minister Louis Farrakhan**

   - Louis Farrakhan 1972 Soul! Interview

     https://www.youtube.com/watch?v=37fykZ8xwPY

- Louis Farrakhan FULL Interview | Breakfast Club Power 105.1 | June 5, 2015

  https://www.youtube.com/watch?v=kH_funhYwwM

2. **Dr. Boyce Watkins**

   - Dr. Boyce Watkins Interview at The Breakfast Club Power 105.1 (03/26/2015)

     https://www.youtube.com/watch?v=x9D80AhZLVM

   - Dr. Boyce Watkins - Blacks must start their own Businesses

     https://www.youtube.com/watch?v=OXR87oBW63c

3. **Dr. Michael Eric Dyson**

   - Point Loma Writers: An Evening with Michael Eric Dyson

     https://www.youtube.com/watch?v=MlXITjn0Ngo

   - America as Post-Racial or Post-Racist:Michael Eric Dyson

     https://www.youtube.com/watch?v=ksFx4tnWP1A

4. **Dr. Cornel West**

   - The Gifts of Black Folk in the Age of Terrorism - Pt 1

     https://www.youtube.com/watch?v=hd__axmkEMw

   - "Niggerization of America" - Cornel West

     https://www.youtube.com/watch?v=bEScONfKqFk

5. **Dr. Marc Lamont Hill**

   - Crown Forum: Empowerment & Orientation

     https://www.youtube.com/watch?v=z9a9CWsrGEE

   - Marc Lamont Hill Address NAACP

     https://www.youtube.com/watch?v=XamriYi8clU

Freedman's Bank

https://en.wikipedia.org/wiki/Freedman's_Savings_Bank

https://www.youtube.com/watch?v=OxCGBaaHpqs

How to write a scholarly article

1. **A Step-by-Step Guide on Writing a Scholarly Paper**

   http://www.csudh.edu/phenom_studies/study/guide/guide.htm

2. **How to write a Research Article**

   http://www2.archivists.org/sites/all/files/How_To_Write_a_Research_Article_FINAL.pdf

3. **Writing your First Scholarly Article**

   http://bibliomining.com/nicholson/firstarticle.htm

8th grade writing ideas

1. **Writing Prompts**

   http://www.writingprompts.net/8th-grade/

2. **Writers Notebook Prompts**

   http://www.internet4classrooms.com/grade_level_help/writing_using_prompts_language_arts_eighth_8th_grade.htm

How to Write a College Admission Essay

1. **9 essay tips to "wow" admission officers**

   http://college.usatoday.com/2014/10/23/9-essay-writing-tips-to-wow-college-admissions-officers/

2. **Top 10 tips for writing a College Essay**

   http://www.nacacnet.org/studentinfo/articles/Pages/Top-Ten-Tips-for-Writing-a-College-Essay-.aspx

3. **Sample College Admission Essay**

   http://www.internationalstudent.com/essay_writing/college_essay/

African American Historical Figures

1. **African-American Firsts: Government**

   a) **Local elected official**: John Mercer Langston, 1855, town clerk of Brownhelm Township, Ohio.

   http://www.biography.com/people/john-mercer-langston-9373265

   b) **State elected official**: Alexander Lucius Twilight, 1836, the Vermont legislature.

   http://www.biography.com/people/alexander-lucius-twilight-213035

c) **Mayor of major city:** Carl Stokes, Cleveland, Ohio, 1967–1971. The first black woman to serve as a mayor of a major U.S. city was Sharon Pratt Dixon Kelly, Washington, DC, 1991–1995.

http://www.biography.com/people/carl-stokes-37578

d) **Governor (appointed):** P.B.S. Pinchback served as governor of Louisiana from Dec. 9, 1872–Jan. 13, 1873, during impeachment proceedings against the elected governor.

http://www.biography.com/people/pinckney-pinchback-9440897

e) **Governor (elected):** L. Douglas Wilder, Virginia, 1990–1994. The only other elected black governor has been Deval Patrick, Massachusetts, 2007–

http://www.biography.com/people/douglas-wilder-39254

f) **U.S. Representative:** Joseph Rainey became a Congressman from South Carolina in 1870 and was reelected four more times.

http://www.britannica.com/EBchecked/topic/489920/Joseph-Hayne-Rainey

g) **The first black female U.S. Representative** was Shirley Chisholm, Congresswoman from New York, 1969–1983.

http://www.biography.com/people/shirley-chisholm-9247015

h) **U.S. Senator:** Hiram Revels became Senator from Mississippi from Feb. 25, 1870, to March 4, 1871, during Reconstruction.

http://www.biography.com/people/hiram-r-revels-9456129

i) Edward Brooke became the first African-American Senator since Reconstruction, 1966–1979.

http://bioguide.congress.gov/scripts/biodisplay.pl?index=b000871

j) Carol Mosely Braun became the first black woman Senator serving from 1992–1998 for the state of Illinois. (There have only been a total of five black senators in U.S. history: the remaining two are Blanche K. Bruce [1875–1881] and Barack Obama (2005–2008).

http://www.biography.com/people/carol-moseley-braun-205626

k) **U.S. cabinet member:** Robert C. Weaver, 1966–1968, Secretary of the Department of Housing and Urban Development under Lyndon Johnson;

http://www.biography.com/people/robert-weaver-9525780

l) **The first black female cabinet minister** was Patricia Harris, 1977, Secretary of the Department of Housing and Urban Development under Jimmy Carter.

http://www.biography.com/people/patricia-roberts-harris-205630

m) **U.S. Secretary of State:** Gen. Colin Powell, 2001–2004.

http://www.biography.com/people/colin-powell-9445708

n) The first black female Secretary of State was Condoleezza Rice, 2005–2009.

http://www.biography.com/people/condoleezza-rice-9456857

o) **Major Party Nominee for President:** Sen. Barack Obama, 2008. The Democratic Party selected him as its presidential nominee.

http://www.biography.com/people/barack-obama-12782369

p) **U.S. President:** Sen. Barack Obama. Obama defeated Sen. John McCain in the general election on November 4, 2008, and was inaugurated as the 44th president of the United States on January 20, 2009.

http://www.biography.com/people/barack-obama-12782369

q) **U.S. First Lady:** Michelle Obama became the nation's first black First Lady when her husband, Barack Obama, defeated Sen. John McCain in the general election on November 4, 2008

. http://www.biography.com/people/michelle-obama-307592

r) **First African-American Republican woman to serve in the House:** Ludmya Bourdeau "Mia" Love won her race in Utah in the 2014 midterm elections.

http://www.biography.com/people/mia-love

2. African-American Firsts: Law

a) **Editor, Harvard Law Review**: Charles Hamilton Houston, 1919.

http://www.biography.com/people/charles-h-houston-9344795

b) Barack Obama became the first President of the Harvard Law Review.

c) **Federal Judge:** William Henry Hastie, 1946;

http://www.greatblackheroes.com/government/william-hastie/

d) Constance Baker Motley became the first black woman federal judge, 1966.

http://www.biography.com/people/constance-baker-motley-9416520

e) **U.S. Supreme Court Justice:** Thurgood Marshall, 1967–1991.

http://www.biography.com/people/thurgood-marshall-9400241

f) Clarence Thomas became the second African American to serve on the Court in 1991.

http://www.biography.com/people/clarence-thomas-9505658

3. African-American Firsts: Diplomacy

a) **U.S. diplomat:** Ebenezer D. Bassett, 1869, became minister-resident to Haiti;

http://diplomacy.state.gov/discoverdiplomacy/explorer/peoplehistorical/169797.htm

b) Patricia Harris became the first black female ambassador (1965; Luxembourg).

http://www.biography.com/people/patricia-roberts-harris-205630

c) **U.S. Representative to the UN:** Andrew Young (1977–1979).

http://www.biography.com/people/andrew-young-jr-9539326

d) **Nobel Peace Prize winner:** Ralph J. Bunche received the prize in 1950 for mediating the Arab-Israeli truce.

http://www.biography.com/people/ralph-bunche-9231128

e) Martin Luther King, Jr., became the second African-American Peace Prize winner in 1964. (*See* King's Nobel acceptance speech.)

http://www.nobelprize.org/nobel_prizes/peace/laureates/1964/king-bio.html

Must See Black Documentaries

1. The African Americans: Many Rivers to Cross
2. Freedom Riders
3. Slavery by Another Name
4. Eyes on the Prize
5. The Black Power Mixtape 1967-1975
6. Soundtrack for a Revolution
7. Dark Girls
8. The Black List: Volume One
9. Breaking The Huddle: The Integration of College Football
10. More than a Month

NOTES

....

....

....

....

....

....

NOTES

_____

_____

_____

_____

_____

_____

_____

_____

NOTES

9th Grade Curriculum

Introduction

Congratulations, your child is officially a high school student! This grade is an important transition as your child begins their college preparatory journey and start preparing for college scholarships. Most high schools give students the opportunity of selecting their own classes for the first time in their educational career. It's important that they make good decisions because it could directly affect their college acceptance. The social aspect of fourteen and fifteen year olds being integrated with students who are older and more physically and mentally mature is huge. Parents play a crucial role in this transition because students can become so overwhelmed that they become frustrated and don't perform to their full capabilities. Parents must maintain constant communication with the school counselor and other members of the child's support team to keep him or her engaged.

KEYS POINTS

- Get Involved In School Activities
- Career Assessments
- Read 30 minutes daily
- Continue Developing Writing Skills
- Develop Oratorical Skills

9th grade the students should:

1) Read Everyday

2) Get Involved At School By Joining Clubs And Organizations

3) Talk To Family About Future Plans

4) Find A Mentor

5) Learn How To Ask For Help

6) Take Challenging Courses

7) Seek Out People In The Career They Want To Be Involved

8) Take the Preliminary SAT (PSAT)

ACT Preparation Material

1. https://www.number2.com/

2. http://www.4tests.com/act

3. http://www.princetonreview.com/college/free-act-practice-test#!practice

4. http://www.actstudent.org/sampletest/

5. http://www.sparknotes.com/testprep/books/act/

SAT Preparation Material

1. http://www.veritasprep.com/free-sat-resources/

2. http://www.proprofs.com/sat/

3. http://ineedapencil.ck12.org/

4. http://www.princetonreview.com/college/free-sat-practice-test#!practice

5. https://www.khanacademy.org/test-prep/sat

Apps To Help Excel At Math

1. Algebra Touch ($2.99)

2. Brainscape (Free)

3. Khan Academy: PreCalculus (Free)

4. Mathematical Formulas ($.99)

5. Ooops (Free)

6. Quick Graph: Your Scientific Graphing Calculator (Free)

Science Apps

1. Ultimate Dinopedia ($4.99)
2. Earthviewer (Free)
3. Anatomy 4D (Free)
4. Netter's Anatomy Atlas (Free)
5. Star Walk (Free)

Career Assessments

1. **Career Test**

   http://www.educations.com/career-test

2. **Strong Interest Inventory**

   https://www.cpp.com/products/strong/index.aspx

3. **Career Assessment Inventory**

   http://www.pearsonclinical.com/talent/products/100000574/career-assessment-inventory-the-enhanced-version-cai.html

4. **Holland Code Career Test**

   http://www.truity.com/test/holland-code-career-test

Personality Indicators

1. **Myers-Briggs Type Indicator (MBTI)**

   http://www.myersbriggs.org/my-mbti-personality-type/mbti-basics/

2. **Jung Typology Test**

   http://www.humanmetrics.com/cgi-win/jtypes2.asp

Current Notable Scholars

1. **Melissa Harris-Perry**

   - Melissa Harris-Perry On Being Black In America Today

     https://www.youtube.com/watch?v=PSsJJZ8cZ-k

   - Sister Citizen: Shame Stereotypes and Black Women In America

     https://www.youtube.com/watch?v=blX2YHdqUJA

2. **Dr. Imani Perry**

- Justice Works 2014 Keynote Address

  https://www.youtube.com/watch?v=H2j6h-V7CkM

- Black Heritage Month Assembly

  https://www.youtube.com/watch?v=TqX2EmiTXsM

3. **ricia Rose**

- How Structural Racism Works

  https://www.youtube.com/watch?v=T5b3DJMBmic

- Lund-Gill Lecture 2014

  https://www.youtube.com/watch?v=Twck8lKMuHM

4. **Angela Davis**

- How Does Change Happen?

  https://www.youtube.com/watch?v=Pc6RHtEbiOA

- Angela Davis California Prison Interview, 1970

  https://www.youtube.com/watch?v=8sLIDscuc-M

5. **Dr. Eddie S. Glaude Jr.**

- Preaching With Power 2012 Lecture

  https://www.youtube.com/watch?v=IR-rXJsOlcU

- African American Identity

  https://www.youtube.com/watch?v=sRVeEt03wy8

Public Speaking

1. **Why Is Public Speaking Important**

   http://writingcommons.org/index.php/open-text/genres/public-speaking/844-why-is-public-speaking-important

2. **Why Speaking Proper English Is Important For Your Career**

   http://www.exforsys.com/career-center/english-vocabulary/why-speaking-proper-english-is-important.html

3. **6 Reasons Why Public Speaking Skills Are Important**

   http://squirrelers.com/2012/07/30/6-reasons-why-public-speaking-skills-are-important-to-career-and-finances/

How To Write A Scholarly Article

1. **A Step-by-Step Guide on Writing a Scholarly Paper**

    http://www.csudh.edu/phenom_studies/study/guide/guide.htm

2. **How to write a Research Article**

    http://www2.archivists.org/sites/all/files/How_To_Write_a_Research_Article_FINAL.pdf

3. **Writing your First Scholarly Article**

    http://bibliomining.com/nicholson/firstarticle.htm

9th grade writing ideas

1. **Narrative Writing Prompts**

    http://www2.asd.wednet.edu/pioneer/barnard/wri/narr.htm

2. **Writing Prompts for High School Students**

    http://www.brighthubeducation.com/high-school-english-lessons/100463-original-writing-prompts-for-your-students/

How to Write a College Admission Essay

1. **9 essay tips to "wow" admission officers**

    http://college.usatoday.com/2014/10/23/9-essay-writing-tips-to-wow-college-admissions-officers/

2. **Top 10 tips for writing a College Essay**

    http://www.nacacnet.org/studentinfo/articles/Pages/Top-Ten-Tips-for-Writing-a-College-Essay-.aspx

3. **Sample College Admission Essay**

    http://www.internationalstudent.com/essay_writing/college_essay/

NOTES

....

....

....

....

....

....

NOTES

NOTES

10th Grade Curriculum

Introduction

Now that your child has had a year to settle into the high school arena, their sophomore year should be smoother than their freshman year. It's very important that parents continue to provide structure, set limits, enforce consequences and give rewards when deserved. If your child plans to attend college then taking the Preliminary SAT exam (PSAT) is very important during this school year. The scores on the test can lead to National Merit Scholarships and give the student an indication of how they will perform on the actual SAT. Just in case your child is not interested in going to college, in this section we offer other career opportunities for them to explore.

KEYS POINTS

- Preliminary SAT
- Tips For Preparing For College
- Vocational Careers
- How To Speak Clearly
- How to Write A Book

10th grade the students should:

1) Read Everyday

2) Get Involved At School By Joining Clubs And Organizations
3) Talk To Family About Future Plans

4) Find A Mentor

5) Learn How To Ask For Help

6) Take Challenging Courses

7) Seek Out People In The Career They Want To Be Involved

8) Take the Preliminary SAT (PSAT)

ACT Preparation Material

1. https://www.number2.com/

2. http://www.4tests.com/act

3. http://www.princetonreview.com/college/free-act-practice-test#!practice

4. http://www.actstudent.org/sampletest/

5. http://www.sparknotes.com/testprep/books/act/

SAT Preparation Material

1. http://www.veritasprep.com/free-sat-resources/

2. http://www.proprofs.com/sat/

3. http://ineedapencil.ck12.org/

4. http://www.princetonreview.com/college/free-sat-practice-test#!practice

5. https://www.khanacademy.org/test-prep/sat

6 Apps To Help Excel At Math

1. Algebra Touch ($2.99)

2. Brainscape (Free)

3. Khan Academy: PreCalculus (Free)

4. Mathematical Formulas ($.99)

5. Ooops (Free)

6. Quick Graph: Your Scientific Graphing Calculator (Free)

Science Apps

1. Ultimate Dinopedia ($4.99)
2. Earthviewer (Free)
3. Anatomy 4D (Free)
4. Netter's Anatomy Atlas (Free)
5. Star Walk (Free)

Reasons to Take the PSAT

http://www.schoolguides.com/reasons_to_take_the_psat.html

1. **3 Reasons Your PSAT Score Matters**

http://www.usnews.com/education/blogs/college-admissions-playbook/2013/09/23/3-reasons-your-psat-score-matters

Vocational Careers

http://www.reviews.com/vocational-careers/

1. **27 Highest Paying Jobs That Requires No College Degree**

http://www.trade-schools.net/articles/highest-paying-jobs-without-degree.asp

2. **8 Highest Paying Vocational Careers**

http://www.insidermonkey.com/blog/8-highest-paying-vocational-careers-314588/

How to Be an Effective Communicator

1. **Julian Treasure**

- How To Speak So That People Want To Listen

https://www.youtube.com/watch?v=eIho2S0ZahI

Understanding Student Loans

http://www.nerdwallet.com/blog/nerdscholar/understanding-student-loans-real-terms/

1. **Understanding Student Loans 101**

http://www.learnvest.com/knowledge-center/understanding-student-loans-101/

2. **Types of Student Loans**

   https://www.salliemae.com/plan-for-college/types-of-student-loans/

3. **Understanding Repayment**

   https://studentaid.ed.gov/sa/repay-loans/understand

How to write a Book

   http://www.writersworkshop.co.uk/how-to-write-a-book.html

1. **How to write a Book: 3 Practical Steps**

   http://www.writersdigestshop.com/how-to-write-a-book

2. **How To Write A Novel**

   http://www.how-to-write-a-book-now.com/how-to-write-a-novel.html

Motivational Speeches

1. **Eric Thomas**

   - **Secret To Success**

     https://www.youtube.com/watch?v=sl_kv-6-I_s

   - **You Owe You**

     https://www.youtube.com/watch?v=7Oxz060iedY

   - **Don't Be Outworked**

     https://www.youtube.com/watch?v=95L0mqHKve4

How to Write a College Admission Essay

1. **9 essay tips to "wow" admission officers**

   http://college.usatoday.com/2014/10/23/9-essay-writing-tips-to-wow-college-admissions-officers/

2. **Top 10 tips for writing a College Essay**

   http://www.nacacnet.org/studentinfo/articles/Pages/Top-Ten-Tips-for-Writing-a-College-Essay-.aspx

3. **Sample College Admission Essay**

   http://www.internationalstudent.com/essay_writing/college_essay/

NOTES

....

....

....

....

....

....

NOTES

11th Grade Curriculum

Introduction

Aside from academics and extracurricular, 11th grade is also about being proactive. Considering that your child has a year before graduation, there's still a lot of things that must be completed. Students should continue the process of reading daily, practicing writing skills through various mediums and becoming a better public speaker. In this section we will offer information and tips about how students should dress for success, taking the ACT, options on paying for college, tips for 11th grade, how to screen and script write and how to create a short film.

KEYS POINTS

- Dress For Success
- Take The ACT
- Decide How You Will Pay For College
- Tips For 11th Grade
- Screenwriting
- Scriptwriting
- How To Create A Short Film

In the 11th grade the student should:

1) Read Everyday

2) Get Involved At School By Joining Clubs And Organizations

3) Talk To Family About Future Plans

4) Learn How To Ask For Help

5) Continue Taking Challenging Courses

6) Seek Out People In The Career They Want To Be Involved

7) Take the ACT

Tips to Navigate Thru 11th Grade

1. Study for ACT in the Summer

2. Write College Essay

3. Ask for Teacher Recommendations Early

4. Avoid Taking A Lot Of Test In May

How to Create a Short Film

https://www.youtube.com/watch?v=PalEaciHvXI

1. **How to Write a Short Film**

https://www.youtube.com/watch?v=sWbZZdmSCD8

How to Write a Screenplay

https://www.youtube.com/watch?v=7ykCCvT5mG4

1. **Scriptwriting for Beginners**

https://www.youtube.com/watch?v=NJO1wyuAIpw

How Will You Pay For College?

1. **How to Pay for College and not go Broke:**
   a) Scholarship Search

   b) Summer Savings

   c) Obtain College Credits while in High School

   d) Get Involved with your School and Community

   e) Get the Best SAT/ACT Score Possible

   f) Fill out the FAFSA

g) Apply to a number of Colleges

h) Compare College Award Letters

i) Negotiate the Best Award Package

j) Prepare a Budget with Your Family

k) Save Graduation Gift Money

l) Take Federal Work-Study

m) Borrow Federal Student Loans

n) Get a Part-Time Job or Paid Internship

o) Get Good Grades

p) Continue your Scholarship Search

q) Borrow Private Student Loans

r) Use Student Discounts

s) Stick to your Budget

Dress For Success

1. **8 Tips To Dress For Interview Success**

   http://www.forbes.com/sites/lisaquast/2014/01/27/8-tips-to-dress-for-interview-success/

2. **5 Tips to Improve Your Look For Your Job Interview**

   http://www.careercast.com/career-news/dress-success-5-tips-improve-your-look-your-next-job-interview

3. **10 Tips For Dressing For Success**

   http://www.careerfaqs.com.au/news/news-and-views/top-10-tips-for-dressing-for-success/

Les Brown

1. **You Gotta Be Hungry**

   https://www.youtube.com/watch?v=t-V8dg0BkAQ

2. **Life Has No Limitations Except The Ones You Make**

   https://www.youtube.com/watch?v=_nkT46Dc_U4

3. **It's Possible**

https://www.youtube.com/watch?v=W6nT2yFc5UA

NOTES

....

....

....

....

....

....

....

....

NOTES

_____

_____

_____

_____

_____

_____

_____

_____

NOTES

_____

_____

_____

_____

_____

_____

_____

_____

12th Grade Curriculum

Introduction

Aside from graduation and prom, 12th grade is also about being focused on building a great future. Becoming a lifelong self–learner is the key to long term success. Remaining educated of what's trending in the market is professional development at its best. Choosing a profitable major is crucial but so is pursuing what you are passionate about. Your child is about to enter a world of possibilities.

10 KEYS POINTS

1. Take time to think about what you like to do; dream and imagine ideal careers.
2. Challenge yourself in high school, but don't overwhelm yourself.
3. Work, volunteer, or otherwise gain some experience.
4. Get as much education as you can.
5. Talk with as many adults as possible about careers and colleges.
6. Remember that everyone must follow his or her own path in life.
7. People change; don't feel locked into any college or career now
8. Don't let anyone control your dreams and ambitions.
9. It's never too early nor too late to get organized and begin making plans.
10. Never stop learning… read, grow, and expand your mind.

What is Coding?

http://www.codeconquest.com/what-is-coding/

7 Easy Ways to Learn Coding and Computer Science for Free

https://dailytekk.com/6-easy-ways-to-learn-coding-and-computer-science-for-free/?reading=continue

Pack It Up: What to Bring to College

http://www.fastweb.com/student-life/articles/pack-it-up-what-to-bring-to-college

TIPS to Succeed In College

1. Attend classes.
2. Study 3-5 hours per day
3. Join a study group
4. Use tutors
5. Choose a major you love.

Suggested Readings

1. The New Jim Crow: Mass Incarceration in the Age of Colorblindness by Michelle Alexander
2. A Question of Freedom: A Memoir of Learning, Survival and Coming of Age in Prison by Avery Trade-Penguin Group Books
3. Post Traumatic Slave Syndrome: America's Legacy of Enduring Injury and Healing by Uptone Press
4. Countering the Conspiracy to Destroy Black Boy Vol I & II by Jawanwa Kunjufu
5. Lord of My Land: 5 Steps to Homeownership by Jay Morrison
6. HIP HOP 2 HOMEOWNERS: How WE Build Wealth in America! by Jay Morrison
7. For colored girls who have considered suicide, when the rainbow is enuf: a choreopeom by Ntozake Shange
8. The Metamorphosis by Franz Kafka
9. Nobody: Casualties of America's War on the Vulnerable, from Ferguson to Flint and Beyond by Marc Lamont Hill
10. 10) Fences by August Wilson

How To (Really) Become A Millionaire Through Real Estate

https://www.forbes.com/sites/brandonturner/2016/10/18/4-things-you-need-to-become-a-millionaire-through-real-estate-investing/#d40e6f0247ad

Seven Tips on How to Build Long-Term Wealth with Rental Properties

http://homeguides.sfgate.com/seven-tips-build-longterm-wealth-rental-properties-90535.html

NOTES

....

....

....

....

....

....

NOTES

_____

_____

_____

_____

_____

_____

_____

_____

NOTES

71983324R00100

Made in the USA
Columbia, SC
08 June 2017